Caroline Wyatt.
Christma

1993

A CHILD'S EYE VIEW
1904–1920

Wirksworth, Derbyshire, May 1902. Grandma Wilkins' birthday. Joyce aged 3 months on Mother's knee with Father behind. Dorothy aged 3 years far left of picture. Uncles, Aunts and Cousins

A CHILD'S EYE VIEW
1904–1920

Joyce Wilkins

The Book Guild Ltd.
Sussex, England

The Book Guild Ltd.
25 High Street,
Lewes, Sussex

First published 1992
© Joyce Wilkins, 1992

Set in Baskerville

Typesetting by Raven Typesetters
Ellesmere Port, South Wirral

Printed in Great Britain by
Antony Rowe Ltd.
Chippenham, Wiltshire.

A catalogue record for this book is
available from the British Library

ISBN 0 86332 744 3

CONTENTS

LIST OF ILLUSTRATIONS

ACKNOWLEDGEMENTS

I acknowledge with gratitude the encouragement given to me by the present Headmistress of my old school to write the memories of my schooldays, and the interest shown by my family and friends, without which this book would never have been published.

Dorothy aged 4 years, Joyce aged 8 months

PREFACE

My father's diary for the year 1909 opens at a page for each week of the year. On the left-hand sheets there are seven spaces to note down the events of each day, while on the opposite pages there are spaces for the diarist to record anything that is relevant. In father's case the right-hand pages were used to record each day something for which he could give PRAISE TO GOD.

On looking through the diary eighty years after it was written I turn to January 1909. On Tuesday 19 January the subject for PRAISE was 'That we were able to have tea at Walthamstow Hall when Joyce entered, and Dorothy returned as boarders today.' On Wednesday 20 January was recorded 'Farewell meeting (Lantern lecture) Sevenoaks,' and PRAISE 'for the splendid attendance and kindly spirit manifested at the farewell meeting tonight'. On Thursday 21 January 'Joyce's birthday'. PRAISE 'That Miss Hare was so pleasant and thoughtful when we took the children to the school for the last time'. Friday 22 January 'Sail for India in SS. Egypt'. PRAISE 'For the contingent of Christian Endeavourers who saw us off at Sevenoaks station'.

This is the adult's record of events that had affected me very deeply, so I decided to write 'A Child's Eye View' of these same days, and of my childhood from my earliest memories up until the time I left school and 'put away childish things.'

This book is the result.

Mission Bungalow No. 1, Berhampur, where Dorothy and Phyllis were born

Mission Bungalow No. 1, Cuttack, where Eric Gordon was born

1

Berhampur, Ganjam, India 1904

Drip! Drip! Drip! . . . Drops of rain falling rhythmically through the roof of the verandah had made a little puddle on the floor. The child was alone, with no one to stop her, hopping. Hop! Hop! Hop! . . . Over that little puddle she went. the puddle grew larger. Now she couldn't hop over it any longer, but now she had to jump. Jump! Jump! Jump! . . . Over she went from one side of the water to the other. Her sandals got wet, and then of course it happened. Her foot slipped as she landed, and she fell over backwards, and splashed into the puddle and banged her head on the verandah floor! And she yelled! Ayah came running, and picked her up, scolding her as she did so, and Mother called anxiously from the bedroom where she was nursing the new baby sister, and all was noise and commotion and cries of 'You naughty girl!' The bump on her head was examined, and the agitated exclamations suggested that she would seriously damage her brain if she kept knocking her head like that, and what a stupid thing it was to do, to try to jump over a puddle of water.

I was two-and-a-half years old at the time that this happened. My sister Dorothy was nearly six, and now there was this new sister, Phyllis, who had taken my place as 'baby' of the family, and was taking up all Mother's attention.

Mother's anxiety was expressed in anger towards Ayah and me, and it left me with a deep feeling of guilt. I was a 'naughty girl' who was always causing trouble to Ayah, and always banging her head and damaging herself. Ayah was patient with Joycie-baba, and bore the brunt of the complaints about my behaviour.

One day, during the rainy season there was a terrific hailstorm, with hailstones 'as big as pigeons' eggs' battering down on the roof, and Ayah ran out into the rain and picked up one of the biggest hailstones and placed it in the palm of my outstretched hand. How it burned and tingled as it gradually dissolved into water!

The verandah had plants in pots all round the edge, and the frogs would collect there in the corners, in the cool shade by the pots and under the palm leaf matting, and sometimes there might be a snake there too. Once there was a hornet's nest built in the corner of the verandah, and Dorothy came across it, and was badly stung. She received so much loving care and attention due to the stings, that I went to look at the nest for myself, and was also stung. Now I was scolded as a 'naughty girl' because I had been told *not* to go near the nest. Dorothy was stung about the head and face, I had one sting on my cheek I remember, but I shut my eyes and pretended that I could not see because of the sting, and insisted that I could not see to put on my socks. But Ayah 'called my bluff' and I got little sympathy.

My pictures of Ayah are of bare brown feet and the border on the edge of a white sari – a child's eye view from the ground level where I squatted. I remember vividly those patient feet on one particular occasion. Our Grandpa had given to each of us a little china plate. Mine was green and Dorothy's was blue, and one day I dropped my plate and it broke. The grown-ups expressed so much regret and sorrow at this piece of careless-ness that in anger and fear I took up a stone and, squatting beside those patient brown feet that stood near me, I smashed up the broken pieces of crockery and ground them to powder in the dust of the compound. I wonder if the reason for my great distress then was that Grandpa had just died? He died in 1905 when I was three years old.

I seemed frequently to be 'careless' and to break things, and the act was always accompanied by deep feelings of guilt and despair.

We had 'week-day' toys, which were put away on Saturday nights, and 'Sunday toys' which were kept in a drawer during the week and only brought out on Sundays. There was that Sunday – I think it was not long after Phyllis-baba was born – when we were to go to the churchyard to put flowers on the little grave of the baby brother whom we had never known. He had died before Dorothy was born. But another baby had died not long ago, he was Alan Jarry, Edna and Gordon's baby brother. Were we all going together to the cemetery, four children and two Ayahs? It certainly was a special outing that we were taking. We had on our best Sunday clothes and we carried our best Sunday dolls. I had mine in my arms – a baby doll in long clothes and with a veil over her face to protect her from the sun. I was 'careless' and I dropped her and she was broken. Irate voices over my head – 'You naughty girl!' 'See what you have done!' Waves of guilt, fears – and a kind of satisfaction? Did we go to the cemetery that day? Memory cannot recall, but the feelings of guilt remain.

There was a little rag doll to which I was devoted. His name was Punchy. He had a red jacket and blue trousers, and a cap with bells, and turned-up shoes with bells on the toes. Punchy went everywhere with me, until one day when he was missing. We hunted high and low. He was nowhere to be found. I was heart-broken. And then we saw Mr Jarry coming across the compound from the Boys' Orphanage next door. With him came his son Gordon, who was about my age and hanging from Gordon's hand was a soaking wet Punchy whose colours had run. Mr Jarry looked stern but there was a flicker of a smile at the corners of his mouth. Gordon looked defiant – 'I was only baptising Punchy' he explained as he handed over the wet doll. I was delighted to have him back, but he was never quite the same again.

There were two Mission Orphanages in Berhampur in which boys and girls whose parents had died in a dreadful famine in 1903 were housed and fed and clothed and educated by missionaries of the Baptist Missionary Society. Mother superintended the Girls' Orphanage, which was under the direct care of the Indian matron, Rhoda. Mr and Mrs Jarry had charge of the Boys' Orphanage. These 'famine orphans' were now well-nourished and cared for, and were educated and given a chance in life, but people sometimes referred to them scornfully as 'rice Christians.' There was a stile between the two compounds. We were not supposed to talk to the boys in the Orphanage, but sometimes when we were going to school in the Jarrys' bungalow, I would pretend that I couldn't climb over the stile and one of the boys from the orphanage would come and help me. I never told about these 'escapades'!

Mrs Jarry's sister was a teacher and she was staying with

them for some months, and while she was there we had lessons with her. Her name was Miss Moody, and while Edna and Gordon called her Aunt Jane, Dorothy and I called her 'Auntie-Miss-Moody'. Dorothy and Edna were reading words, while Gordon and I were just learning to write and to name our letters. Alan, their baby, had died and Phyllis our baby was too young to come to school.

Father was a busy missionary working in his study for several hours each day, often with a *pundit*, translating the Bible into Oriya, writing, preparing sermons, and then going away on preaching tours in the villages round about. We children did not see a great deal of him as we were with Ayah, and Father used to say then, and also repeated later in life, that 'Children ought to be born three years old as they are not of much interest to their fathers before that time'!

I can only remember once being punished by him, I cannot now recall for what misdemeanour I was to be smacked, but Mother was urging him to punish the naughty child, and Father was trying to 'smack my bottom'. He had hold of my hand and I hung in the air with my feet off the ground, squirming and wriggling and trying to get away from the large heavy hand that was slapping me. I was howling at the top of my voice and was deeply affronted by the indignity of being slapped by Father. I don't remember Mother ever slapping me – if she did it was probably just a quick slap on my hand and soon forgotten.

Ayah was the one who looked after me, and she had to be patient and try to cajole me into good behaviour, for she was the one who would be scolded for not controlling me when I was naughty.

Then there was my real Auntie, Mother's sister, Auntie Florrie, who was also a missionary. She was kind and loving, and would draw pictures for us and tell us stories, and she had a couple of striped squirrels that were allowed to run up and down her person and make a nest in her hair. We loved her but we did not see a great deal of her, as she worked in the Zenana Mission in Cuttack while Father was stationed in Berhampur. Auntie Florrie died soon after I left India to go to school in England. I had a feeling as a child that she would have been a more approachable and 'better' Mother than the one we had. I spoke of this many years later to one who knew the two sisters well and she scoffed at the idea and said that Florrie was a typical Victorian spinster. The child somehow knew differently.

Grandpa was also a missionary. I saw him once or twice in my early years. He was a kindly old man, with a grey beard. He had married twice, and Nana, his second wife, was Mother's stepmother. Grandpa died in 1905 after many years of service with the Baptist Missionary Society, and two of his daughters and a son carried on the family tradition as missionaries.

Mother had spent her early childhood in India, but when she was twelve she was sent 'home' to school in England. Walthamstow Hall in Sevenoaks was a school for the daughters of missionaries, and at that time was run with strict Victorian discipline under the Headmistress, Miss Unwin. Mother only had four years schooling there, for when she was sixteen her mother died and she and her two sisters were called back to India to look after their Father and the younger children. My Grandma had died in childbirth, and her ninth baby had died with her. Grandpa did not marry again until after two of his daughters, Edith and Nellie, had married. He then married Fanny Miller, whom we knew as Nana.

Nana used to tell us that she and her sister Jessie had attended the same school that Mother went to, Walthamstow Hall, but they were at Walthamstow before the school moved to Sevenoaks. Fanny's and Jessie's parents, Mr and Mrs Miller were missionaries, and Nana said that when they first came out to India they sailed in a sailing ship and the voyage took six months. When Fanny and Jessie left school they joined their parents in India. Jessie married a missionary, Mr Percy Heberlet, and they had three daughters. Their youngest daughter, Elsie, married our Uncle Harry Pike, and I was a bridesmaid at their wedding. Fanny had married our Grandpa and so was our Mother's and Uncle's stepmother. When Father came out to India as a missionary he met Nellie Pike, Grandpa's youngest daughter, and they were married in 1895.

Because of the death of her mother with the sad loss of the new baby, it is not to be wondered at that our Mother was fearful of pregnancy and childbirth. Years later she told me that Dr Nina Ottmann, who attended her when four of her children were born, had told her that she should never have had children – but she had five. The first baby a son, was born when Mother had typhoid fever. All the attention was centred on saving the mother's life, and the baby apparently was somewhat neglected. I think his was a premature birth, and he only lived for ten hours, though he might have survived had he been given special care. Father never ceased to mourn the loss of his son, and his hopes for another were dashed three times as daughters were born. We all felt that we were a disappointment to him, and this was confirmed when in 1907 at last another son was born.

Mother's fears and anxieties extended to much that she saw in the world around her in India. She was continually afraid of finding snakes behind the plants on the verandah or in the bathroom, she was afraid of finding scorpions in our shoes or tree frogs clinging to mosquito nets over our beds. And these things happened. She was frightened of spiders and insects and creepy-crawlies and, in later years, we teased her that she gave the surname 'Killit' to every small creature that invaded the house – 'There's a spider, kill it.' 'There's a beetle, kill it!'

The world outside was even more hostile, and she tried to shield us from the sights and smells and sounds in the bazaar. 'Don't look! Shut your eyes! Hold your breath! Don't touch! Come away!' sounded constantly in our ears. 'What are those dogs doing?' 'Come away! Don't look! – they are being naughty.' And then the dreadful cries of pain as laughing boys threw stones and interrupted mating dogs . . . 'What's the matter with that lady? Has she been hurt?' as a woman with blood stains on her sari and holding a new-born infant in her arms begs for money from passers-by . . . 'That man's got a spotty face.' 'Come away, quickly!' as a man with smallpox mingles with the crowd in the belief that to get rid of it he must pass the disease on to others.

In the bazaar you would see groups of men carrying their dead on open litters to the burning *ghats* on the river bank. You could be accosted by beggars whose features were eaten away by disease, lepers without toes or fingers, children so deformed that they could not walk but dragged themselves along the ground, the blind, the sick, the maimed all crying out for attention or *poisa* (pence) . . . but we 'mustn't look, mustn't touch, mustn't listen' Not that our parents were hard-hearted or callous. They were there to serve the people, they sacrificed their lives to preach to the heathen, and to minister to the orphans. They gave money and food to the poor and needy. Each week, on a certain day, little piles of *pice* were put out in rows in the compound, and the lepers would come and collect them, and would be given food and loin-cloths too. The coins that they handled were tainted (all coins, particularly coppers, were suspect and had to be handled as little as possible, and the hands washed afterwards), and the stile that the lepers came over to enter the compound should not be used by us until it had been cleaned up after the lepers' weekly visit. Danger lurked everywhere.

Animals were suspect too. 'Pi-dogs' (pariah) that roamed the bazaar were not to be touched, jackals seen in daylight near to the houses brought the fear of rabies. Brahminee bulls stalked through the bazaar, eating what they liked from the stalls unhindered by any, and mounted half-starved cows as they wandered among the crowds. Old women sat by the roadside with small undernourished calves to which they gave a handful of grass if any passer-by threw a small coin to them. Thus the calf received some food, the old woman 'earned' her living, and the giver of the coin assured for himself 'credit' in the after-life.

The foods displayed on the stalls in the market were not for us of course. 'Don't touch! Don't eat that!' The fruits and sweetmeats looked so tempting but were also tempting to flies.

The whole world outside seemed to be hostile and dangerous, and we must shut ourselves away from it.

But it was not only strangers that frightened me. Many of the older missionaries filled me with awe and fear, perhaps because I sensed Mother was in awe of them too.

There was Mrs Bond whom Mother referred to on many occasions and frequently quoted. 'Mrs Bond says . . .' Mrs Bond was very fat, and very, very old and she always dressed in black. She had a black-and-tan terrier called Nita who had a flat, black back like a table, and wheezed and waddled when she walked. I was frightened of Nita and hated her because once when I had found a nest of new-born mice in the go-down, and was carrying them carefully indoors on a piece of cardboard, Nita came and jumped at me and knocked the mice out of my hand, and then she stood there and crunched them up and ate them before my eyes, and took no notice of my loud protestations. Horrid dog!

17

And Mrs Bond was also an object of fear and horror in my mind because of a song that someone had once sung to me. It went like this:

'Oh what have you got for dinner Mrs Bond?
'There's beef in the larder and ducks in the pond.
Dilly, dilly, dilly, dilly, come and be killed,
For you must be stuffed and my customers filled.'

We used to see chickens being caught by the cook and killed for dinner. I once saw all the servants sitting round in a circle laughing at a chicken that was running round in eccentric circles with its throat cut and its neck all twisted before it finally fell down dead. It was a horrible sight and I felt guilty for looking when I knew that I wasn't supposed to see it, and for eating the chicken afterwards at dinner.

Another person of whom Mother stood in awe was Doctor Nina Ottmann. She was a dark Eurasian woman of German or Dutch extraction who worked in the Mission Hospital. She was also a very large and stout woman, and she expressed her opinions strongly.

When I was little I used to lisp slightly, pronouncing 'j' as 'th'. 'I'm thest (just) going to do it,' and my own name as 'Thoycie'. Dr Ottmann decided that I was 'tongue-tied' and one day, without warning, made me open my mouth, and then she cut the fraenum under my tongue with a pair of scissors! She then gave me a large sweet to suck, I remember, though my mouth was full of blood! I never trusted her after that.

Then there was Mrs Jarry. She was a friend of Mother's, but they never called each other Nellie or Aggie, nor did we call Mrs Jarry 'Auntie'. Mother was always concerned about 'What Mrs Jarry would think' and 'What Mrs Jarry would say'. She was a Scot and a trained nurse, and a stern disciplinarian following a strict missionary code. Her sister 'Auntie-Miss-Moody' was very much more gentle and easy-going, but somehow I believe it was Mrs Jarry and not her sister who sang the chorus of a hymn, with actions, which almost gave me nightmares! The actions were rolling the arms, with the elbows bent, round and round towards yourself, while you sang

18

'Over and over like a mighty sea
Comes the love of Jesus
Rolling over me!' (Clasp your arms round yourself.)

This was supposed to be comforting, but I was frightened of
the sea – I hated it – and this chorus terrified me!
From Berhampur the sea was a few miles away at Gopalpur,
and we went there sometimes for a holiday. We went by bullock
cart, with 'trotting bulls', and stayed in the Mission Bungalow.
The garden was acres of sand with tall cactus-like plants with
huge spikes of giant lily-of-the-valley-like flowers (yucca?).
On one holiday the Long family and the Jarrys were all
there together, so there was Daisy, Archie, Gracie and Ivy
Long, Edna and Gordon Jarry, and Dorothy, Phyllis and me.
There we all were playing in the sand, while Phi-ba was in
Mother's or Ayah's arms. The three fathers had been very busy
digging a huge hole in the sand and building up the walls of a
sand-castle, and we children were paddling in the hole when an
extra large wave crashed over the castle wall and flooded the
hole and drenched us all! The bigger children jumped out, but
the wave swept Ivy and me off our feet! How we howled! What
a commotion! There was laughter from the fathers, screams
from the mothers, and spluttering terror and tears from us
young ones who thought that we were going to be drowned!
Mrs Long was particularly concerned about Ivy who was her
baby and seemed to be in real danger. I was three years old,
and I was scolded for crying and making such a fuss, as I was 'a
big girl now'. But I was really frightened.
That summer, in June 1905, Grandpa Pike died in Cuttack
and his widow, Nana, decided to retire and return to England.
Dorothy was nearly seven and it was time for her to go to
school, so here was the opportunity for her to travel with Nana.
Father was transferred to the Mission Station in Cuttack, and
we left the Jarrys at Berhampur.
Just before she sailed away across the sea to an unknown
country and an unknown life at school in England, Dorothy-
baba was heard speaking in fluent colloquial Oriya and
explaining to a tearful Ayah that she was going across the
ocean, which, she said – opening her arms wide – 'contained
SO MUCH water that NO MAN could tell of it.' '. . . Jete pani
achi jey khoibaccu nahi!' A terrifying thought!

May 1906 in Cuttack
Joyce aged 4 years 4 months
Phyllis aged 1 year 10 months

2

Cuttack, Orissa, India 1906–1908

In Cuttack we lived in Nodia (Coconut) Bungalow, a large thatched house with four bedrooms, each with its own bathroom, wide verandahs back and front, and two main rooms in the centre of the house connected by archways. There was a large tank (which would be called a pond or even a lake in England) and beautiful deodar trees, and flame-of-the-forest, and acacias in the compound. (I think it was in Berhampur that we had cork trees. How we loved it when the long trumpet-shaped, sweet scented cork flowers fell from the trees at the end of the rainy season, and we picked them up and made garlands of them and knew that the 'cold weather' had come!) There were more flowers in our garden in Cuttack, and bougainvillae growing over the porch in the front of the house. Nodia Bungalow had a big compound and backed on to the *maidan* so we saw much less of the bazaar than we had seen in Berhampur.

The rooms in the bungalow were large and airy, and there were *punkas* stretched across each one. (This was before the days of electricity and electric fans.) Mother had decorated the dining-room and the drawing-room *punkas* with stencilled leaves and ferns in stippled work. This was done by fastening the plant material on the cloth in a decorative pattern and then splattering over it drops of Indian ink by means of a tooth-brush and comb. When the leaves were removed their image remained. Mother's efforts were much admired by the grown-ups and we children thought that she was very clever to do such pretty work.

The tree-squirrels ran up and down the *punka* ropes and across the tops of the *punkas* and didn't mind that it was only 'pictures' of leaves. What they *did* mind was when they started

21

to build a nest in the corner of the room and it was immediately knocked down.

In addition to the squirrels there were always *jhitipitties* (small house lizards) running up and down the walls of the rooms, and eating the mosquitoes and flies that came in when the lamps were lit. Our house was not fly- nor mosquito-proofed then, as it was later. We slept under mosquito nets at night, and the *punka-wallas* were paid to pull the ropes and gently fan us and try to keep us cool in the hot weather.

Mother had an upright grand piano in the drawing-room and a harmonium in the dining-room. Once when the harmonium would not sound properly Mother found a clutch of *jhitipitti's* eggs in the works. She got them out and put them on the table, and they burst open and tiny lizards ran off in all directions!

Mother played a harmonium in chapel for English service on Sunday evenings, and sometimes for the Oriya service on special occasions. Otherwise the congregation sang unaccompanied in Oriya, and I think on the whole they preferred to do so than to be controlled by the harmonium, as then they were free to repeat verses and choruses as many times as they liked, and to speed up or slow down 'as the spirit took them', and to clap and give a real performance.

Mother found this disconcerting and irritating, she liked to know what she was doing, and that she was leading the singing in an organized and predictable manner.

We children loved singing, either in English or Oriya. We sang with Ayah and we sang with Mother and Daddy. We had a hymn book called *Joy Bells*, and when we were little we each had our own copy. I loved my book, because of the word 'Joy'. I loved all hymns that had the word 'joy' in them or 'rejoice' – especially 'again I say rejoice!' because of my name, and I sang the words out loudly.

'Joy bells ringing, children singing.
Fill the air with music sweet!
Joyful measure, endless pleasure,
Make the sounds of Heaven complete.
Joy bells, joy bells, never, never cease your ringing,
Children, children, never, never cease your singing!
List! List! the sound that swells!
   Joy bells! Joy bells!'

When Daddy was at home and we sang as a family we would sing hymns such as *Onward Christian Soldiers* and march round and round the room in single file after him, all singing lustily.

There is a story that was told by the grown-ups, but I hardly remember the occasion except for hearsay. Apparently one day Miss Barras, a missionary lady, called to see Mother who was, I think, busy at the time with the baby, and Phyllis and I were sent out to give Mother's apologies and say that she would not be long. I must have been five and Phyllis three years old, and we followed Mother's message by asking our visitor if she would like us to sing to her, and then hand in hand we sang (to the best of our ability) 'All Hail the Power of Jesu's name' to the 'curly' tune of Diadem.

'Cra...a...a...wn Him Crown Him! Crown Him!
And Cra.......wn Him Lord of All!'

Phi-ba and I missed our big sister Dorothy-baba. Dorothy used to have her fair hair brushed and tied back in a bow behind her head. I had a parting in the middle and a bow on each side, and Phyllis had her hair parted on one side with one bow. I remember on one occasion brushing my hair back from my forehead and making Ayah tie it at the back, as Dorothy's had been done. I then went into Daddy's study and stood silently beside him while he was working. Presently he looked up and asked me what I wanted. I said 'Guess who I am.' Of course he couldn't guess until I told him. 'I'm not Joycie, I'm Dorothy', and he played along with me for a time. I suppose that I wanted to be the eldest, the important one in the family. And Dorothy who had left us seemed to be more important than ever as letters came from her, and from Nana about her.

Before she had left for England Dorothy and Edna had each had a big rag doll, beautifully made and dressed by Mother and Mrs Jarry. I was envious of Dorothy's doll, called Edna Mary, and sorry that she had been taken to England by Dorothy. They were living with Mother's Aunt Lucy in Enfield. In the household there were some boy cousins, several years older than Dorothy, and years later I heard from her tales of how they used to torment their poor young cousin. One boy, Frank, would stand at the top of the stairs and the other boy, Roy, at the bottom and they would throw poor 'Edna Mary' to each other while the distracted seven-year-old Dorothy dashed up and down trying to catch her beloved doll. At the time I knew little about my big sister's life in England until I saw her again when I came to school, when she was nine and I was six. She spent several months with Aunt Lucy before being sent to school in Sevenoaks in September 1906.

Phyllis and I had no school to go to in Cuttack, and no other children to play with. We had Auntie Florrie with her squirrels, and the other ladies in the Zanana Mission House, but I cannot recall as much of those years in Cuttack as of the earlier ones in Berhampur.

Mother was busy with the 'crochet women'. She gave out fine crochet cotton, and crochet hooks and patterns for beautiful d'oyleys and lace collars and edgings, and the Christian women did fine crochet work at home. Each week they came with their finished work and were paid for what they had done, and more cotton was given out. So some badly needed cash was earned by the women, and the fine d'oyleys, with the lace collars and edgings and insertions which were then worn on dresses and underwear were sent to England and were sold for the benefit of the Missionary Society. It was quite a lucrative business and benefited all concerned.

What else do I remember? Being vaccinated on our arms, which not only 'took' but also 'took bad ways' with enormous boils which then had to be lanced. Father's Mother disapproved of vaccination and paid fines in England rather than let her children suffer this 'unnatural' treatment. In consequence Father had never been vaccinated until he came out to India and nursed a colleague who died of smallpox. He then suffered himself to be vaccinated, and his arm became so infected that they feared that he might lose it, or his life. Thankfully he recovered, though he had a very bad time.

One excitement in 1907 was the appearance of Halley's comet – which I did not see, because I refused to look at it! It was like this. Some time previously there had been an eclipse of the sun and Ayah told me that a dragon was swallowing the sun, and unless Rama came to save us from the dragon we would all live in perpetual darkness. What joy there was when the sun returned! And now here again was some mysterious appearance in the sky which everyone was talking about. Then one night I was awakened from sleep and brought out to look at

24

it. It was all too much for me. I was in Daddy's arms and I hid my face in his shoulder, and in spite of all the excited encouragement from the grown-ups, I kept my face away and refused to look! I was probably told that I was naughty, obstinate, and foolish – but actually I was too frightened to look. I remember that Daddy said I was a silly child, and he told me that I would be *a very old woman* before I had a chance to see it again. And when it returned in my lifetime it could hardly be observed from the brightly lit streets of England – and so I have never seen Halley's comet!

The big event of 1907 was the birth on 30 October of my Father's long awaited son, my young brother Eric Gordon. I remember the day quite clearly. I was five-and-a-half years old, and had been given a toy sewing machine that really worked with a chain stitch. This was to keep me quiet during the day of activity. The baby was born in Nodia Bungalow with Dr Ottmann present and Indian nurses. I sat in the dining-room, sewing. Phyllis was somewhere with Ayah. There was a great deal of excitement and activity in the back bedroom, on the left. Father was working – and probably praying – in his study, off the front bedroom on the right. (In those days it seemed right for fathers to be shut out from being present at the birth of their children; now they are allowed to share in the event.) And suddenly there was the thin cry of a newborn baby! I don't think that I had realised the significance of all the excitement, until that moment. I don't remember noticing my Mother's condition when she was pregnant. Questions were never asked or information volunteered in those days on matters of birth and 'where do babies come from?' Mother did not even discuss her pregnancy with friends. It was 'not done' even among women friends to discuss these matters.

But when the child was born, then all was joy and gladness. The Indians were very free in offering their congratulations that at last the Sahib had a son. There had been little cause for celebration, in fact sometimes only condolences, at the birth of three daughters. But at last Father could speak about 'my son'. Yes, I was jealous, very jealous at times, and especially so as the time drew nearer for my own departure for England and school. That took place in April 1908, but before that there are certain things that I can recall.

The first was a big disappointment on Christmas Day that

year. On Christmas morning I woke very early and saw a pillow case hanging outside my mosquito net. Oh how I longed for a baby rag doll like those that had been made for Dorothy and Edna! Alas! My biggest present was a large picture postcard album which I had for years and never found any use for. The disappointment was so great that I cannot remember what other present I got that year.

My greatest excitement was being asked to be bridesmaid to Auntie Elsie Heberlet on her marriage to Uncle Harry Pike. They were married in Sambalpur on 13 February 1908. I was just six years old. I had a pale grey silk frock, with a yoke with a pocket hanging by ribbons from it, and a big frilly hat, and I carried a basket of artificial flowers. The marriage took place in a Mission bungalow, with Mrs Heberlet, the bride's step-mother, playing the harmonium. I stood proudly behind the bride throughout the service, holding her gloves and her flowers, but young Kitty Heberlet cried and ran to her mother and hid her face in her lap while she tried to play the harmonium. I thought that Kitty should be punished for such behaviour, but no one scolded her. She was such a pretty little girl, and her hair hung down in ringlets, while mine had been tightly plaited when wet and was all frizzy. Another disaster was that the bridegroom in his excitement spilled his cup of tea down the front of my dress, and I feared that I should be scolded because of the stain. Mother was not at the wedding. She was in Cuttack with Phyllis and the baby. I suppose Father took me to Sambalpur. When I got back I tried to describe to Mother the beauty of Kitty's ringlets, cupping my hands to show how the hair was coiled, and Mother just said, 'Yes dear. I know. I know', and I couldn't believe that she could know what ringlets were, for I had never seen anything like them in my life. Uncle Harry gave me a little gold brooch with a horseshoe on it, which I had for many years.

All the family went to Chapel on Sunday mornings. Sometimes it was an English service, and sometimes it was in Oriya. There was also an Oriya service in the afternoon and a service in English in the evening. I think that the chapel was in the same compound as Nodia Bungalow, certainly it was not far away. Mother and Father went to the Sunday evening service too, Father to preach and Mother to play the harmonium, leaving Ayah to give us our supper and put us children to bed. At Sunday supper we often had custard in beautiful individual cut-glass goblets, which had been a wedding present to Mother. I think they were really intended to be used as wine glasses, with the bigger ones to be used for champagne, but as ours was a teetotal household they were put to other uses. (Eighty years later some of these goblets still remain in use, and are much treasured.)

The Ayah who was with us at this time was called Emily. She was a Christian and she and I shared a secret that Mother and Father did not know. Emily Ayah had learned to speak – and so of course could understand – English. Mother always spoke to her in Oriya, and normally we all did the same, but on Sunday evenings when we were alone with her in the house, and the rest of the servants were off duty, Emily Ayah would speak to us in English. And on those Sunday evenings, before I went to school, Emily Ayah taught me Augustus Toplady's hymn 'Rock of Ages, cleft for me.' Verse by verse each Sunday I repeated it with her until I knew each line by heart. The version that she taught me was the original one, but my childish understanding substituted some incorrect (and to an adult) meaningless words and phrases, but I have never forgotten that hymn in the version that I learned it when I was six years old. It had a horrid fascination for me, with feelings of terror conveyed by the imagery and an awful sense of guilt for my own wickedness and for the fact that I was deceiving Mother by speaking to Ayah in English.

This is how I understood the words. the punctuation and spelling indicates the meaning I gave to them, and the italics show the difference from the modern and earlier versions of the hymn.

'Rock of Ages, cleft for me,
Let me hide myself in Thee
Let the water and the blood
From thy *riven* side which flowed (now 'wounded')
Be of sin the double cure,
Cleanse me from its *guilty power* (guilt and power)

Knot the labour of my hands (tie a knot in all I try to
    do)
Can fulfil *MY Lord's* demands (Thy laws demands)

27

Could my zeal no respite know
Could my tears for ever flow
All for sin could not atone,
Thou must save and Thou alone.

Nothing in my hands I bring
Simply to Thy cross I cling
Naked look to Thee for dress (deep sense of shame)
Helpless look to Thee for grace,
Fowl I to the fountain fly (picture of a chicken)
Wash me Saviour or I die (the dying chicken)

While I draw this fleeting breath,
When *mine eyelids burst in death* (now, 'my eyelids close
   in death')
When I *saw the* realms unknown (soar to)
See Thee on Thy judgement throne,
Rock of Ages shelter me,
Let me hide myself in Thee.'

The time was now drawing near for our departure to
England, and for me to go to school. I was the only one of us
born in England. I had been born in my grandmother's house
in Wirksworth in Derbyshire while Mother and Father were
'home on furlough'. I had been brought to India when I was
nine months old, and had always been told I was seasick
throughout the voyage. Father and Mother were also bad
sailors and so I was not looking forward with pleasure to the
voyage. 'So much water that no man could tell of it!' Dorothy
had said.

We had a family photograph taken a few days before we left
Cuttack. It was taken by an Indian who was a professional
photographer who was always called upon to photograph
weddings and other social events. I remember the occasion
quite well, and there is at least one copy of the photograph still
in existence. There we are sitting on the steps of Nodia
Bungalow, Father and Mother with Eric on her knee, and
Phyllis by her side, I am sitting on the steps beside Father, with
my mouth open and a look of worry and strain on my face. I
remember the reason for this. I had on a new frock, made
specially for me to wear on the voyage, and put on for the first

time for the photograph. It was a crisp navy blue cotton with white spots, and I was very pleased with it and felt that it was very smart. The first photograph was taken with baby Eric sitting on my knee. Perhaps he cried and spoilt the picture. I don't know. I don't think there is a copy of that photograph still to be seen. What I *do* know is that he wet himself while sitting on my knee, and wet my new frock and me too! And there I am, sitting with my hands clutching the folds of my new frock in my lap, trying to hide the damp patch in case someone will see it and scold me for spoiling my new frock. That accounts for the look of anxiety and pain on my face while Eric smiles on Mother's knee.

We had a party to say farewell to other missionaries and Indian friends. There were Indian sweetmeats and I had a 'joke' sweet in the shape of a red chilli with a green stalk. When I had eaten the sweet part I tried to eat the stalk, but it was not intended to be eaten and tasted very nasty, so I went in search of some water to drink to take the taste out of my mouth. The glass jug containing the boiled drinking water was on a shelf, and I put my hand up to take it down and pour out some water, when to my horror I saw it contained a large *jhittipitti*. The poor creature had fallen into the vessel and was unable to get out. Had it drowned, or was it still alive? Its eyes seemed to look accusingly at me, but I could do nothing. The memory haunted me for months.

But another memory of that last evening in Cuttack was deliberately fostered by the servants. They had caught some fireflies and put them (unharmed) under a piece of fine green gauze in the centre of the dining table so that we could enjoy the beauty of a living table decoration. We were urged to look at them carefully – the little blue-green lights flashing under the gauze –and to remember the sight, for, they said, we would not see fireflies in England.

And that night we left for Calcutta, to take a ship for England.

3

On the SS Syria *bound for London, April 1908*

Cuttack railway station was on the main line between Calcutta and Madras, but its situation was such that most of the main trains arrived at Cuttack during the small hours of the morning, and we were accustomed to getting up in the middle of the night if we had to catch a train.

We children had been put to bed early in Nodia Bungalow, and we had slept for a time before being awakened in the middle of the night, wrapped in coats and bundled into *tikka-gharies* (horse-drawn cabs) for the drive to the station. Here amidst all the noise and bustle, still half asleep, we were put to bed once more, now on the bunks of a railway carriage, where we soon fell asleep again as we started on the long journey to Calcutta.

The events of the next couple of days, spent in the train and then in the Mission House in Calcutta remain a blank in my memory as do the scenes of bustle and activity which we must have experienced when we finally went aboard the *SS Syria* and set sail for England.

The first thing that I remember on the ship is being taken down to a playroom for children on the lower deck, where there was a stewardess in charge. Mother was unpacking our luggage in the cabin, Father was looking after Phyllis, and I was told to 'look after baby' in the playroom. There was a baby's swing on ropes. It had a square seat, with ropes at each corner, and two slats of wood on each of its four sides, which could be pushed up and down on the ropes. A baby could sit up comfortably in the swing, safely wedged in on all sides so that he couldn't fall out. And so sat my baby brother, and I was told to swing him. He seemed to enjoy this, but when the engines started and the ship turned and moved slowly down the

Hoogley and out to sea, and she began to heave slightly, my head began to feel queer, and I did not enjoy the sensation.

There is a strange smell on board a ship always, and this was particularly noticeable at bath-time that night. Our baths in India were taken standing on the floor of the bathroom in a sort of sink with a hole for the water to drain away (and for the odd snake or frog to enter the bathroom). We had a large earthenware pot full of cold water, and a kerosene tin of hot water (which had simply been heated by standing in the sun all day) and, as we stood there Ayah soaped us all over and then poured water over us – and that was a bath. Here on board ship we went into a cabin which had a big bath in which we sat. Hot salt water came out of a tap, and there was a jug full of fresh water to use with the soap, as the soap would not lather in salt water. And as we sat in the bath the motion of the ship could be seen as well as felt as the water splashed up and down or from side to side. And my head felt very queer indeed.

I don't remember if we were all in the same cabin. I suppose it could have been a four berth cabin, with, in addition, a baby's cot. My memories of the voyage are very blurred because I became very ill, with a high fever. But before that happened there are one or two incidents that I can still vividly recall.

I was standing on deck and looking at the swirling water in the wake of the ship, and to my horror I saw bobbing up and down a number of children's toys, dolls, teddy bears and woolly animals that a small, angry, unhappy little boy had taken from the children's playroom and thrown overboard. My heart sank, and an awful fear struck me. What if I should throw my baby brother overboard? Of course I was jealous of him, and I did not want the responsibility of looking after him when Mother was sick and I was feeling sick too – but the awfulness of the thought made me feel almost as guilty as if I had committed the deed.

And the poor, unhappy small boy – his story was a tragedy. I cannot remember his name, but the grown-ups were always talking about him, and he was a constant source of anxiety. He was not travelling with his parents –why I do not know – but I believe that he was with comparative strangers who were taking him home to England, and he was, as they said, 'more than we had bargained for'. He was destructive, disobedient,

31

noisy, rude and 'always up to something'. and in the end an awful thing happened to him. He fell down the hatchway and fractured his skull, and had to be put off the ship when she called at the next port so that he could go to hospital. I don't know for sure what happened to him after that, but his injuries were so bad that I believe he must have died. Poor child! What a terrible state of mind he was in, and what a terrible physical consequence! And what a burden of fear he passed on to me.

A few days after we left Calcutta the ship berthed in Colombo, and we all went ashore for several hours. We went to see a missionary family and spent the day with them. After they had given us a meal Father and Mother stayed to talk to their friends and Eric, who was only six months old, of course stayed with them, but we children were sent off to play. I am not sure whether the Colombo missionaries had a daughter as well as a son, or whether the other child with us was Phyllis, then under four years old. It is the boy that I remember though I cannot recall his name. He was probably a little older than I was, about seven or perhaps eight, and was very forceful and bossy. If he had a younger sister she is now just a shadowy figure in the background. I don't think there was even an ayah present.

The boy showed us all his possessions and organised all the games we played, and then finally all was set up for him to astonish us with some conjuring tricks. He had a set of painted clay or wooden fruit – a banana, a mango, and also I think there was a custard apple or a guava. He performed various tricks, by sleight of hand apparently making them disappear from one place and reappear in another. He was not particularly clever, but his patter and quickness of hand fascinated me. Then he started to do suggestive and vulgar things with the banana by sticking it in the front of his trousers. Finally he pretended to eat the banana, and then, with a great show of straining and effort, to produce it from under him as if it were passing out from his 'back passage'. I half believed that he had really eaten it when he said that he had, and then he showed me the fruit which had specks of red paint on it, and told me that this was blood that had come out from his body. I was horrified and frightened. I knew that grown-ups would not like it if they saw us playing such 'dirty games', and I was so disgusted by all that was said and implied by his actions that the thought of eating bananas was revolting!

32

(This incident wasn't the only reason for my dislike of bananas, it was also because my baby brother was being weaned on mashed bananas, and I had to feed him with this revolting mess when I was feeling seasick.)

So we returned to the ship after the day ashore, and were soon on the way again to England. I don't remember much more about that journey, however, because I developed high fever and spent the rest of the voyage seriously ill and confined to the cabin. At first it was thought that I was suffering simply from a bout of malaria, but as my temperature remained dangerously high for a long time the ship's doctor decided that I must be moved to another cabin. There was a two-berth deck cabin available and I was moved into it. I suppose it was still in the second class section of the boat – as missionaries we were not travelling first – but it was certainly more airy and spacious than the cramped cabin on the lower deck. Here I was nursed night and day by Mother, a stewardess, and Mrs Jarry. It was fortunate that Mrs Jarry, a nurse, was there. She and her husband were on the same journey, taking Edna and Gordon home to school.

It turned out to be fortunate that Gordon was there too, for he came to my rescue. It is a story I have often heard told, but I hardly remember the incident myself because I was barely conscious. Apparently the lock on the door slipped when, for a short time, I was alone in the cabin, and nobody could get the door open. They sent for the ship's carpenter to take the lock off the door, when someone had the bright idea of using a small boy to get through the porthole. As it was a deck cabin this was quite possible, and Gordon Jarry was hoisted up and pushed through the porthole, and he was able to unlock the door from inside. I think I have a vague, shadowy recollection of this happening, but perhaps only because I have heard the story recounted.

What I do remember is being subjected to an ice-pack. My temperature continued to be dangerously high, and none of the drugs in use in 1908 seemed able to reduce it, so it was decided to use drastic methods. Mrs Jarry and the stewardess gave me an ice-pack. I was tightly wrapped in sheets that had been soaked in ice cold water, and then lumps of ice were packed all round me, and a rubber bag filled with ice was placed on my forehead. It was all done with a sternness and no-nonsense attitude on Mrs Jarry's part, and I lay there, shivering and whimpering in those wet sheets and felt that I was being punished for all my wickedness. I don't know how long it lasted, but I believe that the drastic treatment was effective and that my temperature was brought down. I was left in a very weak state, and I told the girls at school, later, that I had become quite a baby and had had to learn to walk again.

At the very end of the voyage I remember a conversation that I had with the ship's doctor. All through my illness I had refused to speak to him, and on this last day he tried once more to break down the barrier of my silence. He kept asking me what my name was, and I still refused to answer. Then at last he said, 'If you tell me your name, then I will tell you mine.' This seemed to me to be a fair exchange, and so I said, very quickly, 'Joyce Lucy Wilkins', and he replied 'W W Wyngate Saul', I have never forgotten it! When I first went to school I used to dance about (having first 'learned to walk again') shouting 'W W Wyngate Saul!' and it became a favourite chant.

We sailed into Southampton, but we did not disembark there. Uncle George (W.G.) Father's eldest brother, came on board the ship with the sad news that Grandma Wilkins had died. She had tried to live to see her beloved youngest son again, but had passed away the day before we arrived. Uncle George saw Phyllis on the deck when he came on board and recognized her because of the likeness to Mother, and told her to 'Take me to your Mother, little girl'. Then Uncle George went ashore again, and we sailed round to Tilbury.

Here a grown-up had brought Dorothy to meet us. Was it Nana, or Auntie Lucy, or a mistress from Walthamstow Hall who was with her? I don't know. All I remember is that Dorothy in her excitement had dashed up to a man wearing a sola topee, thinking it was Father, only to be confronted by a complete stranger! Poor child! Of course anyone on the boat might have brought his sola topee with him, but Dorothy hadn't reckoned like that, and Father was wearing a trilby!

I remember the meeting with Dorothy. I was in Father's arms, and looking down on her from a height, but what a *big* girl she seemed. She was nine and I was six. She handed me a bunch of flowers, saying 'The rose in the middle's for Mother.' And then we all came down the gangway – Mother carrying

Eric, Father carrying me, and Dorothy hand-in-hand with her little sister Phyllis.

It was 8 May 1908, and all this noise and bustle and smoke and dirt – was ENGLAND.

4

England – 1908

The atmosphere was heavy with confusion and anxiety when we first landed in England, with grown-ups weeping and discussing in low tones what was to be done now, and we children feeling very lost and bewildered. The first cause for concern was that Grandma's death had changed our plan of going to stay with her at 'The Chestnuts' in Wirksworth (the house where I was born) and we had to make other arrangements. Then, to add to the difficulties, Dorothy had come from school where they were all in quarantine for chicken-pox or some other infectious disease, and it was considered unwise for her to stay with us and run the risk of us all being taken ill. So Dorothy, poor child, had to be packed off back to school in Sevenoaks, and leave us all again so soon after having been united with the family. It was a sad parting. Daddy went off the Derbyshire to be with his brother and sisters and attend his Mother's funeral. And we three children and Mother, where did we stay? I don't remember. Maybe it was with Nana and Auntie Jean Heberlet in Woodford Green, or with Auntie Lucy in Enfield. I don't know. The final arrangements remain a blank in my mind, I only remember the earlier anxious discussion. We found beds *somewhere* for the night, someone must have taken pity on us. Our heavy luggage I suppose was sent to the Mission house.

It must have been difficult to find relatives or friends who could put up two adults and three small children, including a baby of seven months, so I think it must have been very soon that we took a furnished house at 2 Camden Grove, Camden Road, Sevenoaks, and this became our home until Mother and Father went back to India. I am not sure whether we had a landlady or whether we had the whole house to ourselves. I

36

know that we all caught the chicken-pox while poor Mother had shingles quite soon after we got there. Father was very often away from home as the Mission House sent him about the country 'on deputation', preaching each Sunday in different churches aiming to stir up among their members an interest in missionary work and a willingness to give money to the Baptist Missionary Society.

When we all four had chicken-pox Dorothy and Phyllis were together in one bedroom and, at least during the daytime, Eric was with them, and they seemed to be playing games and enjoying themselves, while I was in a small room by myself, again with a very high temperature, and in fear of the tiger that seemed to be lurking behind the dressing table. It must have been an anxious time for Mother, but eventually we all recovered, and life took on an English family pattern, without Ayahs or table-boys or other servants.

I recall one breakfast time. We were all sitting round the table, Daddy at one end with his back to the open French doors which led to the garden in which there was a small shed. Mother was at this end of the table, feeding Eric, Phyllis was sitting beside Daddy, and I was beside Mother. Suddenly Phyllis put down her spoon and said loudly and sternly, 'Stop that roaring, Mr Lion. You are making *much* too much noise!' And then quietly getting on with her breakfast she explained to the rest of the family, 'I've got 52 cattles in that shed, and Mr Lion *will* keep roaring and *I won't have it!*' The grown-ups laughed a bit and played along with her, but I was quite disturbed. What had she got in that shed? What could she hear that I couldn't hear? Could she really see 52 cattle? Phyllis was nearly four and was a child full of fancies, I was six years old and still lived half in the world of fairies.

Eric was a sturdy and very active baby, and he was continually getting into scrapes. When we first arrived he was crawling everywhere and always picking up things and putting them into his mouth, causing Mother to panic for fear he should swallow something unsuitable. He loved to get hold of books too, especially books with nice red, hard covers, and to suck them and to bite them as an aid to teething! Unfortunately the books in the house didn't belong to us, and Mother was dismayed to find baby with red dye all over his mouth and hands and a book with a limp, chewed cover. The grown-ups said that obviously he was going to be a scholar with his liking for books, but they took care to put them out of his reach. Bananas were another passion of his, and Eric stole them whenever he could find them. He would gobble them quickly, but if he heard anyone coming he would put the remains under a cushion and sit on it! Many a squashed half-banana was found under cushions or down the sides of arm-chairs. The sideboard cupboard had a fascination for him too, and when he had learned to walk he would pull himself up by the door of the cupboard and steal lumps of sugar or anything interesting that he could find there. Once it was a pot of 'yellow jam'. He took a big spoonful – and it was mustard! If Mother was cross with him, and if he was punished he would go behind a big arm-chair in the corner of the room and stay there and sulk for a while. Once, I remember, after he had been hiding behind the chair we suddenly heard scuffling and giggling, and when he emerged this time the eleven-month-old baby had found a pair of his Father's boots behind the chair and had thrust his feet into them and was trying to walk in them! Eric had an infectious laugh, and as he grew up he always had a delightful sense of humour.

There was rivalry between us children at mealtimes. We had porridge for breakfast and Daddy would write our names in golden syrup on top of our portions of hot porridge. It wasn't fair Dorothy had seven letters, so had Phyllis, while I had only six letters in my name even if it was spelt as Joycie! Eric couldn't count. Our bread was formed in cottage loaves, and we would call 'bags I' for the little round of crusty loaf on top! It was a normal cheerful, loving, squabbling family.

In the summer after school broke up, and Dorothy could come with us, we went for a holiday to the seaside. I think it was to Worthing. I don't remember much about it except that we all saw our first aeroplane. It flew low over the sands. We were very excited and cheered and waved, but Eric was terrified and cried.

When we came back to Sevenoaks it was time for me to go to school with Dorothy, and so in September 1908 I started my schooldays at Walthamstow Hall. For that first term I was a day girl, but Dorothy had returned as a boarder.

It was a lovely autumn and I can still picture some of those mornings when I walked to and from school passing gardens

The family in England in
1908

full of flowers – michaelmas daisies and dahlias – with the trees turning to autumn colours. These sights were linked with what I was doing at school. With a big brush full of purple paint I was shown how to lay it down flat on the paper, and repeat this, making a circle of petals, and then put a big blob of yellow paint in the middle – and there was a michaelmas daisy! It was magic! I looked at the flowers and at my painting of them and was thrilled to see how perfect each of them was. And then there were the autumn colours of the trees. I was learning a poem at school which I recited with gusto, and on which Miss Livock our kindergarten mistress complimented me, and told the other children to 'listen how Joycie says it'. That was bliss! The poem was about a robin and started, 'Good-bye, good-bye to Summer, For Summer's nearly done,' and one verse had the lines, 'The trees are Indian Princes, but soon they'll turn to ghosts'. I didn't quite understand what it meant but I stood up proudly and imagined that I was a Rajah, and then I shivered and shook like a ghost, and I fed the imaginary robin with crumbs at the end of each verse.

I was learning to knit and to make scarves for my dolls, and I was learning to read from Nellie Dale readers. These were based on a phonetic system which also used colour to help us distinguish between the sounds of the letters. For instance t and p were printed in red together with all the other voiceless consonants, while d and b and the voiced consonants were in blue, the vowels were in yellow, and the silent letters were in green, when the words were introduced. Of course we all learned to recite the alphabet in those days, and with pride I taught my little sister Phyllis to say it too. One day I was allowed to bring this little sister to school with me, and she stood on a chair and recited in front of the class, 'Little brown seed, oh little brown brother'. I had also taught her this poem, I glowed with pleasure! She had learned the alphabet to say as a birthday present for Mother on 21 November, but the full effect of this was slightly spoiled because Dorothy recited it backwards!

We had drill in the gym, marching and doing exercises to music with dumb-bells. (In later years, when we were older, we exercised with Indian clubs.)

On one afternoon Mother came up to school and sat and watched while we had our drill class. I worked very hard,

Walthamstow Hall, Sevenoaks,
as it was in our time

leaping about and trying to impress her and my beloved teacher, Miss Livock. I was very pleased with the effect I was making until that evening at home when Daddy asked how things had gone. Unfortunately by a slip of the tongue Mother made a *Spoonerism* and said, 'Joycie was jumping about like *a hat on cocked bricks!*' and everybody laughed. I was mortified. What was a hat on cocked bricks? Of course I didn't know the phrase 'a cat on hot bricks' and this joke was repeated time and time again when the story was told to other people. So much for my attempt to impress the grown-ups!

As we came near the end of term and Christmas, Miss Livock set us all the task of writing a letter to Father Christmas telling him what we would like to find in our stockings. These letters were written with great care, and then taken to show Miss Hare, the Headmistress. And then, as we had a fire now in the grate in the West Room (our kindergarten room) the letters were all burnt and we ran out into the garden to see the smoke and ashes floating up the chimney! I had asked for a doll with fair hair and blue eyes, and sure enough at the end of term party Father Christmas brought me one. She was rather small, but she certainly had fair hair and blue eyes.

41

5

The Parting – 1909

Father's diary for 1909 shows that we must all have gone up to Derbyshire after the end of term, and were probably there over Christmas, but I have no recollection of a holiday spent with relatives that year. All Father's relations were in and around Derby. His brother W.G. (Uncle George) with his wife Auntie Annie were to be our official guardians while our parents were in India, and his sister Auntie Alice with her husband Uncle Harry at Long Eaton, and another sister, Auntie Elsie with Uncle Tom on their farm at Sawley Grange agreed to have us sometimes during the school holidays, and so did his niece, Mabel Potter, and also Mother's brother Uncle John Pike. There were many uncles and aunts and cousins on both sides of the family but there were no grandparents living who could have ultimate responsibility for our welfare. My cousin Oliver Wilkins (Bob) was at the time a young man of about 19 or 20, who expected to become a successful businessman (and did so). Father used to tell us how Oliver held the young baby Eric in his arms and said to him, 'I'll make the money and you shall spend it on the little Hindus!' This prophecy did at least partially come true. Bob became very wealthy, and Eric became a missionary.

So during that Christmas holiday we must have visited many relatives and stayed in many different homes, and it is strange that no memories of it remain. I was probably too worried and anxious about the coming separation.

On Saturday 2 January, Father gives thanks in his diary 'for a walk with the three children this afternoon, and then tea with them at Mabs''. Mabs was Mabel Potter, Uncle George's eldest daughter. On Sunday 3 January Father records that he preached at the Gospel Hall. This was a Mission that was started by his father, my grandfather, in Victorian times.

Then on 5 January Father writes in his diary 'Returned to Sevenoaks', gives thanks 'for the good send-off from Derby (W.G., Bob, Jim, Uncle Tom and Joe) this morning and the "flag" at Sawley.' (A white cloth was put out to wave as the train for London passed Sawley Grange Farm.)

Then on Friday 8 January the entry gives 'thanks for one more country walk with the children before we are separated.' Poor Daddy! I wish I could remember that 'country walk' and also the 'lantern lecture on the Pilgrim's Progress' on 12 January that Daddy records 'that Joyce and Dorothy enjoyed so much tonight.'

When we come to 19 January he gives thanks 'that we were able to have tea at Walthamstow Hall when Joyce entered and Dorothy returned as boarders today', and then on 21 January the entry is 'Joyce's 7th birthday' and thanks that 'Miss Hare was so pleasant and thoughtful when we took the children to the school for the last time.' The entry on Friday 22 January is 'Sail for India in SS Egypt,' with thanks expressed 'for the contingent of Christian Endeavourers who saw us off at Sevenoaks station.'

It was these last entries in the diary, found among old letters nearly eighty years later, that made me want to write the 'child's eye view' of these events, so baldly stated by the adult, but now re-reading them I have more sympathy for the writer.

I don't remember having tea with Miss Hare, the Head-mistress, the day I entered Walthamstow Hall as a boarder, I was probably too much in awe of her. I do remember Mother taking me up to the night nursery, and kissing me good-night and leaving me there. The nursery had six or eight beds in which the youngest boarders slept. At the time it was under the charge of Nurse Matherson. That night, when Mother left me, I remember that I sat on my bed and howled, and Nurse Matherson sat beside me and in a hopeless attempt to stop my tears copied me, and made faces and cried 'boo-hoo', and hoped it would make me laugh. How I hated her! Surely arms of comfort round a lost and lonely seven-year-old would have been more fitting to the occasion? But the rules of the nursery at that time were 'no nonsense', 'no sentimentality!', 'Pull your socks up!', 'Don't be a cry baby!'

The next day Dorothy and I were taken to Sevenoaks station

to see Mother and Father off. I don't know who went with us, but I have a feeling that it was somebody like the undernurse who was in charge of us.

There was a crowd of people on the platform to wish 'Godspeed' to the returning missionaries, and a hymn was sung and prayers were offered. Dorothy, in her letter to Mother and Father written a day or two after their departure, asks rather plaintively, 'Did you know all the people who came to see you off at the station? I did not, nor the hymn they were singing.'

Then the two sad little children had their final goodbye kisses and hugs, and Mother and Father with Phyllis and Eric boarded the train. The door was shut on them, the guard waved his flag and blew his whistle, and the train started slowly to move. At that moment the full horror of the situation suddenly struck me. Mother and Father were leaving me behind, *and taking Phyllis and Eric with them*. In blind panic I started to run after the train – to stop it, or to climb on board, I don't know which. But I ran, as fast as I could, the full length of Sevenoaks platform and off it and on to the rough stones beside the track, with Dorothy and a porter in hot pursuit. Poor Mother! If she had looked out of the window she would have seen me running along the track after the train. I hope she was spared the anguish.

Of course the porter caught me, and Dorothy, who was not far behind, did her best to restrain and to comfort me. She was then, and she always was, a loving elder sister on whom I could rely. But a very sad tearful little girl was taken back to school that day and left to cry herself to sleep in the night nursery.

There were five or six other children in the nursery when I was first there. I don't remember the exact number as it differed from time to time. The only child's name I recall was that of Kathleen Dauncy who was in the bed opposite mine. She had a slight lisp, and she used to recite when we were in bed at night the poem 'He was a rat, and she was a rat.' She said it with great feeling, and I remember the shiver I felt in the final lines, 'And what befell I never can tell, but they *never* came back again.' There seemed to be an awful foreboding in this.

Each child in the nursery had beside her bed a chair and a washstand, on which were a ewer and basin, a 'bottle-and-up' of drinking water, and a tooth-mug. On the shelf below there stood a chamber pot, and below that there was a deep drawer for dirty linen. I suppose that somewhere in the nursery we had a chest of drawers for our clean clothes, but I cannot picture it. I only remember the washstand so clearly because one day, not long after I had entered the school as a boarder, I opened the bottom drawer of my washstand and climbed into it. I had a feeling that I could curl up in it and close the drawer somehow behind me, and be safe and comfortable inside. But alas! My weight inevitably tipped the whole washstand forward, the ewer and basin fell on me, soaking me with water, and breaking the chamber pot and the bottle-and-up. The noise of the crash brought nurse running in to find out what was happening, and there I lay in a welter of broken china and water. And then there were questions – 'What has happened? What*ever* were you doing? What *were* you thinking of? You stupid child! Are you quite mad?'

What could I say? How could I explain my actions? At the time the reaction of the adults and the other children was bad enough, but it did not stop there. It was a talking point for all with whom I came into contact, especially for Miss Hare. If I met her in the corridor with a visitor she would stop and say, 'What do you think this funny little girl did the other day? She tried to climb into her soiled linen drawer!' And then there would be more questions, and the impression was given that they all thought I was stupid and did very foolish things.

I did another foolish thing in that first spring term. I found a robin's nest in an old tin kettle with one egg in it, and I took the egg and put it in the swing pocket of my frock, with the hope that I could keep it warm and that it would hatch out into a baby robin. But of course it was addled and after a day or two it broke in my pocket, and the smell was *awful*! Again I was a naughty child and a stupid child to do such a foolish thing as to carry a bird's egg in my pocket.

The nursery walls were adorned with huge pictures of Biblical subjects. The pictures must have been about five foot by three foot, and the figures half lifesize. We each claimed as ours the picture that was nearest our bed. There was Daniel in the lion's den over Kathleen Dauncey's bed, I know. There was the Prodigal Son, and the Good Samaritan, and I think that the others were the four men in the Burning Fiery Furnace, and the woman sweeping and looking for her lost coin, but I am not sure of the last two. The one that I am absolutely certain about is the one that I claimed to be mine, and that was the Lost Sheep. The picture was of hills in the distance dotted about with sheep, and a foreground of rocks and shrubs with a little black sheep lying injured and forlorn behind a bush in the bottom right-hand corner of the picture. In the background was the figure of the shepherd climbing down the rocky face to rescue it. The picture was probably called the Good Shepherd, but I thought of it as the Lost Sheep. And I felt such an affinity with that sheep! There was a hymn we used to sing:

> 'There were ninety and nine that safely lay
> In the shelter of the fold,
> But one was out on the hills away,
> Far out from the gates of gold,
> Out in the meadow I heard its cry
> Sick and helpless and ready to die,
> Sick and helpless and ready to die . . .'

In Aunt Fanny's autograph album soon after this my entry stated 'And the little *brack* sheep was me!' Not only was I a black sheep but I could not spell it.

6

Early School Days

My earliest memories of boarding school are of the year in the kindergarten in the West Room with Miss Livock as our teacher. She was a pretty young woman, gay and affectionate, and she used to sing to us when we were at play in the gym. I remember sitting on the floor near the piano and listening enraptured as she played and sang *Loch Lomond* and *My Ain Folk* because of the haunting sadness of the songs. But she could be full of fun and laughter too, and tell exciting stories and act the parts as she told them. She taught us singing games like 'Poor Mary sits-a-weeping' and 'The Farmer's in his den' and, one we loved to play:

'Old Roger is dead and lies in his grave,
Lies in his grave, lies in his grave,
Old Roger is dead and lies in his grave,
Ee. . . ay. . . lies in his grave!
They planted an apple tree over his head. . .
The apples were ripe and ready to drop. . .
There came an old woman a-picking 'em up. . .
Old Roger got up and gave her a clout. . .
Which made the old woman go hippety-hop. . .'

And after the old woman had been chased, she became Old Roger and the whole drama was enacted again.

And then there was 'I sent a letter to my love, and on the way I dropped it, one of you has picked it up and put it in your pocket', with the excitement of racing round the circle when the culprit has been chosen.

Do children still play these singing and acting games, and chant skipping rhymes, and dress up and act stories like the 'Prince and the Swineherd'?

47

Miss Livock brought plenty of fun and excitement into our lives, and she also wrote, in addition to our reports, friendly, newsy letters to our parents, telling them how their little girls, far away across the sea, were settling down.

On the whole my school work went quite well in the kindergarten and I was happy with Miss Livock. I learned to read phonetically but was hopeless at reading and writing words that did not follow that pattern. I did not always pronounce words correctly, and as I had no visual imagery of how words looked, I made wild guesses when writing as to how to reproduce the sounds of my speech. This was before the term 'dyslexia' had been coined to describe 'word blindness', but there is no doubt that I suffered from a form of that particular disorder that has appeared from time to time in different generations of our family, with a marked disability to learn to spell according to accepted practice. This dogged me all my school-days, and I was so frequently held up to ridicule for my mistakes that I developed a sense of anxiety and feelings of guilt out of all proportion to the seriousness of the crime.

I remember once experiencing utter panic when I was attempting to write the word 'donkey', but couldn't remember how to spell it. My mind was a blank. I tried spelling the word aloud, d - o - ng spells dong', but what about the end part of the word? There wasn't a letter for key. I tried *qui* and *kee* but they didn't look right after *dong*. I was in despair as I felt that the rules that I had learned had let me down, and I did not dare ask, 'How do you spell 'donkey?' for fear of being thought stupid.

When I moved into Form I these spelling mistakes were brought sharply to my notice. My dictation was returned with angry red ink marks, and even my transcription, when I had been set to copy from the printed word, had numerous mistakes in it. I was bewildered by it all, and Miss Wood, my new form mistress could not understand it either. How could I be so stupid and careless? I felt lost in the stricter regime of Form I. Our form met in the big Lecture Room, and we sat formally in desks instead of on little chairs and round low tables as we had done in the kindergarten. Now we had 'spelling-bees', and learned to recite our tables, and did mental arithmetic, when the sudden stern question demanding a quick response left me tongue-tied and frightened. Miss Wood accused me of day-dreaming and not trying hard enough. She once exclaimed in exasperation, 'What *is* the matter with you, Joycie? You are wandering about like a lost soul.' A LOST SOUL. To a missionary's daughter the term meant much more than a vague day-dreaming little girl. The full horror of the words sank into my mind with a meaning far beyond what was intended, and they left such a feeling of fear and despair that I have never forgotten them! Miss Wood was not really unkind, but I missed the sympathetic understanding of Miss Livock.

I was no longer sleeping in the night nursery, but now had a little cubicle on my own on the inner side of the Upper South corridor. That meant that the window looked out onto the roof of the Dining Hall and not onto the garden. The cubicle contained a bed, a wash-hand-stand (the same as we had in the nursery), and a chest of drawers for my clothes and toys, and a chair. The wooden partition between it and the one next door was about seven foot high, and we could have our own pictures on it. Mine was an end room, so I had only one wooden partition and a plastered brick wall which had cracks and marks on it which could, with imagination, be seen as pictures of animals and birds. There were sometimes cracks between the wooden planks of which the partitions were constructed, and we could whisper to our neighbour through them, or sometimes we would stand on the bed or dressing-table and converse with the girl next door – but this was strictly against the rules. It was 'NO TALKING in the corridor or in the bedrooms.'

Then there were the noises in the night! We heard mysterious sounds of footsteps along the corridors and knocking on the water pipes. The explanations which satisfied me when I was older were that the floor boards were settling with changes in temperature, which sounded like footsteps, and the knocking was due to air bubbles in the hot water system, but to a small lonely child these sounds were very frightening. I often cried myself to sleep at night with my head under the bedclothes in terror.

Dorothy wrote a letter each week to Mother and Father, and many of these letters are still in existence. I wrote too, and some of mine, written during that first year at school, have been kept also. On 24 June 1909 I wrote, obviously with great care, and with help from Miss Livock:

'My dear Mother. One of the girls gave Miss Livock some tadpoles for our form. I do wish you could come to the play on Public Day. With love and XXX and OOO from Joycie.'

This wish was repeated in other letters, with no idea of how impossible it was for Mother to come from India to see me act as the Prince in our play on Public Day. The drawings on the letter are quite good for a seven year old, especially the 'TORTIS'

On 8 July 1909 I wrote:

'My dear Daddy, We are all having our a examansan and I for reading had 40 and I for niting got 62 bwt I have forgotin the uthers. How in Phyllis in Eric tel tham that I mess tham to play with tham and mess Eric to karry. With love and XXX and OOO from Joyce.'

Whether this letter was not considered good enough I do not know but there is another one of the same date which reads:

'My dear Daddy, How is Eric and how is Phyllis and how is Polly can he talk yet. I like scol very muck. I have broken my comb. I hipe you will like the drawing. I do so want you to come on Public Day. All of us went to Granophone. With love XXX OOO from Joyce Witkins.
(and a page of drawings).

On 19 July 1909:

'My dear Mother. The day before yesterday was Public Day and we had such fun and we form I did out play and Mrs. Ashdown came to woch us. I do so you could come. I hope you will loke the rose that I dree it is my own. Wuith love and a million XXX and OOO to all Phyllis and Eric and Daddy and you. . . .'

The next week I wrote that

50

'We had done our play, Miss Livock sens her love and so dus yer loving doter. . . . Joycie.'

Dorothy wrote in her letter that week:

'I think you will be pleased to hear that I had two prizes on Public Day, one I had was a garden prize and the other was for general improvement. . . We had a lovely day on Saturday (Public Day) Joyce did her part in the play very nicely. . .'

We both felt a great sense of disappointment that we could not have our parents, nor even an aunt or an uncle or a guardian, to be our own 'Visitor' on such days as Annual Meeting and Public Day. Other girls had their Grandma or some relation, even when their parents could not be with them, to share their little excitements and triumphs.

I was frequently in trouble for being late in the mornings, and for being untidy in my bedroom. Life seemed to me to be very complicated, with a continuous rush to obey the sound of bells. I remember the mistress in charge of our corridor, Miss F.L. Bate (whom we called Zephyr because of her quiet sighing voice) trying to improve my timekeeping. She promised me a teddy bear if I managed to be on time in the mornings for a whole month. I made a great effort, and earned, and received a small teddy bear, but I don't think it improved my timekeeping for long. We knew Miss F.L. Bate as 'Flub' too, because of her initials. She had a sister also on the staff, Miss E.B. Bate, who was 'Ebb' - Ebb and Flow. Ebb was very strict, but Flub was very kind-hearted. I remember one Shrove Tuesday when someone mentioned that we ought to be having pancakes. I said with truth, that I had never tasted pancakes. That evening the staff had pancakes at dinner, and afterwards Flub came up to my room, where I was in bed almost asleep, bringing me a pancake on a plate with a slice of lemon and some sugar. It was cold by the time I ate it, and I didn't think much of it if the truth were told, but it was a very kind gesture on Flub's part and showed that she had a real interest in us children.

She and her sister were also daughters of missionaries and had been pupils at the school at the same time as Mother was there. Perhaps that accounted for Flub's understanding, but the strict upbringing they had had when Miss Unwin was headmistress of Walthamstow Hall may have set an example for Ebb to follow. She was a stern disciplinarian, and she tended to use a ruler to rap our knuckles if we misbehaved, or made mistakes in spelling or writing, or played wrong notes in our attempts to play the piano. She made us write our copybooks on alternate pages, first with the right hand and then with the left hand, and woe betide you if your left hand writing was not as neat as your right! I suppose at the time the neurologists were discovering the functions of the two hemispheres of the brain and it was considered advisable to train both sides equally. Baden Powell published *Scouting For Boys* in 1909 and in that book he advocated using both left and right hands for writing and drawing.

One other unhappy memory I have of Miss E.B. Bate was when I was a very new girl, probably in my first term as a boarder. We small children wore white cotton pinafores in the afternoons, and I remember one day that I put my pinafore over my face and head, and I was looking at the view of a strange misty world through the white cotton cloth when suddenly the pinafore was held tightly behind my head so that I was held imprisoned in darkness and could not move. I struggled to get free and eventually the clutching hand released its grip and the pinafore was lifted off my face, and I looked into the grinning face of Miss Bate who had enjoyed the teasing and was enjoying my discomfort. How I hated her, and feared her!

Another struggle that I had in those early days at school was trying to learn to play the piano. As Mother and Father were both fond of making music and Dorothy was having piano lessons at school it was agreed that I should also be allowed to have this 'extra'. I enjoyed singing and could sing in tune, so it was hoped that I would turn out to be musical. But it was not so, in fact it was a disaster!

My first lesson I remember well. It was with Miss Davis, a young pupil teacher, and she took me to have that lesson on the piano in the Reception Room. This was not normally used as a classroom. It was a little sitting room on the right of the front door where girls could meet relations and friends who came to visit them. We were not usually allowed in this room unless we were meeting guests. I don't know why Miss Davis decided to take me there, perhaps it was the only piano available.

52

Anyway, there we sat and Miss Davis introduced me to the keys of the piano. We found the central keyhole and middle C, and I was taught to name the notes as I did a five finger exercise from middle C to G and down again. After about a quarter of an hour Miss Davis told me to sing the names of the notes as I struck each one, and to practise this until I could do it easily, and then she left me. I started to practise, stumping out each note as I struck it with straight stiff little fingers, while I sang its name. Presently the door opened and Miss Hare came in and said 'Oh, it's you, Joycie, is it? I wondered who was making that noise. I don't think you should be in here. Run along now and go to your classroom!' And I thought that I had been doing just what I had been told to do, and Miss Hare called it 'that noise'.

I was never again taken to have a lesson in the Reception Room. I remember having some lessons in the Dining Room where there was a piano and also a clavier. The latter was a silent keyboard on which pupils were expected to practise their scales and exercises without making a sound which could distract others. When I was sent to practise on the clavier I would imagine that I was playing the piano brilliantly before a large audience, and my hands travelled up and down the keys and thumped out chords that only made a dull clicking sound, while I dreamed it was music. The trouble with real piano playing was that I could not make my left hand and my right hand go different ways and each play its own notes. Nor could I remember the tunes that they were supposed to be playing when they had got no words to them.

Miss Davis recognised this difficulty of mine. She remarked that every time I sat down to try to play the little tunes in my 'first steps' music book it was as if I had never seen or heard them before. She suggested that it might make it easier for me to recall them if she wrote words to them, which she did. Then I sang these words as I played, and my right hand could follow the words and play the tune, but my left hand got lost. What a trial I must have been to my teacher, and how disappointed I was myself! But Miss Davis persisted with me and my next book of simple pieces was a little book of songs to be sung while playing. I progressed a little, but it was an uphill struggle for two years, and I did not always have Miss Davis' sympathetic teaching. Other music mistresses struggled to teach me,

1910 in Chesham where Nana lived
before she moved to Woodford. Dorothy 12, Joyce 8

1910 while on holiday with Nana in Chesham

including Miss E.B. Bate. She insisted that my knuckles should remain flat so that a penny could be balanced on the back of the hand while the bent fingers were playing scales. This was hopelessly restricting for me and created more anxiety.

Then in 1911 Mother and Father came back to England, and Phyllis came to Walthamstow Hall. I remember that I was struggling to play a piano piece called *The Enchanted Princess*, but always made mistakes in it, until one day, just before Mother's arrival, I played it correctly right through. My teacher was delighted, and exclaimed with enthusiasm, 'There! You must play it like that to your mother when she comes next week.' I was wildly excited by my success and the prospect of showing off my skill to Mother, but the anxiety was too much for me, and I was never able to play the piece again!

Dorothy was struggling with her music too, but she could play better than I could. She progressed to being able to play *The Policeman's Holiday*, while I never got beyond a few very simple hymn tunes. When Phyllis came to school she started piano lessons and was very soon far and away in advance of both of us. Later she learned to play the violin too, and had special music lessons with Miss Anstey and Dr Edgerton Lowe. She and Eric were very musical.

But this was in years to come. In 1909 and 1910 I was having difficulties with my spelling and with trying to learn to play the piano, and I was adjusting to boarding school life.

7

Life at Boarding-School

You have to learn all kinds of rules of behaviour when you are at a boarding-school such as 'No talking upstairs or in the corridors, and no running in the passages.' It was also 'No talking' in the dining-room when you assembled for a meal until the Headmistress or Mistress-in-Charge had entered and grace had been said. The time spent sitting before the meal was served should be occupied by sewing or knitting. For the purpose of carrying our needlework we made and wore 'lap-bags', like an apron with a large pocket. Of course we did no sewing on a Sunday, so on that day we were allowed to bring a book to the table, but the book must be put aside as soon as the meal began, and then we were allowed to make polite conversation with our neighbour. Every morning we had to learn by heart a verse from a chapter of the Bible and the girls from one Form would be called upon to stand up in turn and recite it. As this was done in alphabetical order I, as Wilkins, usually had time to learn the verse from hearing the others saying it. Woe betide us if we all depended on each other and someone ahead forgot the words! If we were not word-perfect we were sent out to learn it. When a whole chapter of Scripture or a Psalm had been committed to memory, then three girls of different age groups would be called upon by Miss Hare to recite the whole passage. There was no getting away from that.

At the meal there were certain rigid rules to be followed. At breakfast and tea you had to have one slice of brown bread and butter before being allowed to have white bread and jam. We rarely had cake except perhaps on Sundays and special occasions. You must *never* help yourself to anything without it being offered to you, and so you must always be observant of your neighbours' needs and pass them what they require. You might sit with an empty plate, longing for another slice of bread, but your only way of attracting attention to the fact was to ask someone else if they would like some more! We had meat-and-two-veg and a pudding at midday dinner, and we never expected second helpings. The potatoes were boiled in their jackets, and the peel was used by us to hide any unwanted scraps of food on the plate. You were expected to finish all you were given, but sometimes we would leave a sultana or a scrap of food neatly placed in the middle of the plate 'for the dogs or the pigs'. I think this was supposed to be an offering 'to the Gods', but we did not dare to say that!

We followed some unusual traditions. If two slices of bread had not been cut apart but were still joined by a piece of crust we would ask someone to 'have a Philippina' with us, and made a wish as we each pulled the pieces apart. In theory we were supposed to say 'Good morrow, Philippina' on meeting next morning, and receive a gift from our partner, but I don't remember this act ever being completed. We had a great many superstitions concerning gifts. Any girl who was sitting an examination, even an ordinary school examination, and certainly those who were sitting external examinations, was presented with an ordinary pin by each of her friends.

These 'good luck' pins were stuck into the band at the top of her gym tunic, together with pieces of heather, pictures of black cats, horseshoes, and four-leaved clover, and little gollywogs made out of scraps of wool – all mascots whose number and style displayed the popularity of the wearer. Of course we also 'held thumbs' for each other in periods of crisis or anxiety, and had fingers crossed and touched wood as a talisman. The number 13 was unlucky, the number 7 was lucky, we never walked under a ladder on a Friday. Whether we believed all this or not, we took no chances! The Irish girls wore shamrock (sent over from Ireland to Miss Little) for St Patrick's Day, the Welsh were adorned with daffodils (more often than leeks) on St David's Day, and the Scots displayed pieces of tartan or pictures of thistles on St Andrews Day. We English were always disappointed that there were no roses available for us on St George's Day.

Before we had day-girls attending the school we did not have any lessons in the afternoons but were free for a couple of hours to go out for walks, or to play hockey or netball or tennis. When we went out we walked two-by-two in a crocodile, and very often we went to Knole Park through the little gate in Seal Hollow Road known as 'The Hole in the Wall'. Once we were in the park we broke ranks and were allowed to climb the hills (and roll down them), and play in the roots of a big beech tree known as 'the ship'. We were not allowed to go too near Knole House, nor to disturb the deer in the park. In October and November during the rutting season of the deer we were not allowed into the park. On more than one occasion we saw Vita Sackville-West, who was eight or ten years older than I, out in the park.

On Saturdays in the summer and during the Easter holidays we went for long glorious walks to Dunton Green chalk pits, and One Tree Hill, and through beautiful woods and meadows in the Kentish countryside where we picked violets and primroses, bluebells, cowslips, and kingcups in their time.

We had fire-drill regularly so that everyone would know where to go and what to do in case of fire. Sometimes when the fire alarm went we just had to assemble in the right place and answer to roll-call, but occasionally we had a complete fire-drill practice. In the largest cubicles on the top corridors there were canvas shoots stored, and these were to be used as fire-escapes. They were bolted to the floor and folded neatly away under wooden covers. When they were to be used the end of the shoot was flung out of the window and it became a long canvas tunnel. A prefect would then climb into the dark tunnel and with her elbows and knees scraping the sides would gently lower herself, opening up the passageway as she went down until she reached the ground. As soon as she had scrambled out at the bottom a second big girl would follow her, and then a third. When these three girls were out, two would hold the canvas shoot out at an angle from the side of the building, and then one after another all the rest of the girls would slide down the shoot in quick succession to be caught at the bottom as they shot out of the mouth of the tunnel. It was a great thrill! Most people enjoyed the experience except perhaps the prefects who had to go first. Dorothy was one of these. If a small child was frightened of the shoot she would be taken down piggy-back on the back of her school mother. Fire-drills were held fairly frequently but it was only very occasionally that we were allowed to practise the evacuation of the whole school to see how fast we could do it. The exercise was so popular that on one occasion when the fire bell was rung while we were all downstairs at lessons some enthusiastic youngsters rushed upstairs in the hope of going down the fire-escape.

One day in 1915 we had a full-scale fire-drill with the Fire Brigade in uniform with brass helmets and with their fire-engine and ladders. They were testing newly installed fire-hoses, and in the course of the exercise I was carried in a fireman's lift down a fully extended and swaying ladder over the shoulders of a fireman. Dorothy wanted to be the next one to experience this thrill, but Miss Hare put a stop to it. She found the spectacle too nerve-racking.

We did very interesting things in our lessons. We learned a good deal of poetry by heart, and I remember that when I was about eight or nine we learned Longfellow's *The Village Blacksmith*, and one sunny afternoon all the girls in our Form (we must have had very small classes in those days) went with our Form Mistress down St John's Road to the London Road where there was a blacksmith working at his forge. It was a small dark building, and there was a chestnut tree outside it, and we stood in a circle in the room and watched the young man working at his fire, and then we all recited together 'Under the spreading chestnut tree the village smithy stands,' and when we had finished our party piece the blacksmith sang to us. An occasion never to be forgotten.

When we were young we made leaf prints with soot from a candle flame on a greased enamel plate, and took spore prints from toadstools, and printed patterns cut in potatoes. All most exciting! I remember one exciting discovery that I was allowed to make for myself. It was when we were learning about the specific gravity of metals and were told the story of Archimedes and his bath. For homework we were set to find out how to discover how much gold there was in the crown. I thought about it for a long time and when it suddenly dawned on me how it could be done I could have shouted 'Eureka!' too. When we were told in a hygiene lesson that food doesn't just drop down into our stomachs when we swallow, we proved the fact by eating biscuits and drinking milk while we were hanging upside-down on the new wall-bars that had just been installed in the gym. We could swallow the biscuit, but the trouble with the milk was that it tended to come back down the nose when we laughed!

We had just started cookery classes with Miss Heanan in the new cookery school when war broke out in 1914. It was soon found that the school could not afford the possible waste of food by letting us children use up our rations in learning to cook, and so the classes had to become 'laundry work' instead. I learned how to make up the mixture for 'cold water starch' with 'enough candle wax as could lie on a sixpence', which would enable me to starch the stiff collars and shirt fronts that men wore in those days and also the stiff collars and cuffs worn by nurses and parlour-maids. I have never needed to use this knowledge.

Singing classes were a highlight of the week for me, and to sing the sea-shanties and folk songs and patriotic songs that we learned lifted my spirits when I was depressed. I couldn't read music of course, but tonic solfa helped me to sight-read, and when I had learned the tune I sang out so loudly that I was often told to 'shut up' by my form mates. I also enjoyed acting and taking part in the plays and operattas that we performed on Public Days. I should have enjoyed the rest of my lessons but for the constant anxiety I felt about my spelling in my written work, and also the fact that I was so frequently absent through illness. Every term I had one or more spells 'at the Cottage'. When I returned to the class I found it difficult to catch up and to understand what was being taught, and so I tended to day-dream and let it all flow over my head, and got behind in my work.

8

Knole Cottage

Knole Cottage in Holly Bush Lane was about half a mile from the school and had been acquired at the turn of the century to be used as a sanatorium. If we were not too ill when we were 'sent to the Cottage' we would walk down the road carrying our suitcase, but if we were really ill, or the weather was bad, then we were taken down to the cottage in a large, hooded Victorian bath-chair, which was drawn by Emery, the gardener's boy. I spent many weeks of my years at school down at the cottage, and in the first few years that I was at Walthamstow Hall I don't think that I ever had a full term of schooling. In the first year, 1909, Dorothy's letters to Mother and Father frequently gave them information that I was ill. 'May 15th. Joyce has gone to the Cottage today. She had a sore throat and a bad headache. June 5th. Joyce has gone to the Cottage again for the third time with a headache. June 12th. The first Form had their party, but Joyce missed it for she was at the Cottage.' So I missed pleasures as well as lessons.

Knole Cottage was a detached house with I hardly know how many bedrooms, for there were certain parts of the house which we never entered. I think there were four bedrooms in which we children slept, a 'four-legged' room in the front, a double room and a single room at the back, and I think there was also a small single room for anybody who was seriously ill. Mildred Marshall and Beth Piper died at the Cottage during my school-days. There were two staircases, the back stair that we went up and down, and another flight which we never used. I think this must have led to the bedrooms of those in charge of the cottage. I never went into the kitchen which was some-where downstairs, but there was a dining-room also down-stairs, which we used if we were well enough to be up for meals,

62

and another room with a fireplace and a window looking onto the garden. The garden consisted of a few shrubs and a croquet lawn, and a summer house where we could sit when we were convalescent. I don't remember any pictures or gay curtains or anything other than iron bedsteads with white counterpanes, and bed-side lockers. All was plain, without frills, and as hard as the discipline.

Eighty years ago the cottage was run by Miss Ray and Miss Lovett. They were stern 'Christian' ladies, always dressed in black. They called each other 'dear' but treated their charges as if they were naughty little girls for being ill! I believe that Miss Hare deliberately chose those stern people to look after us when we were ill so that there was no danger of us malingering, and no chance of us developing sentimental attachments. I think Miss Lovett did the cooking, and Miss Ray did the nursing. We had to greet her politely and say 'Good morning, Miss Ray' however ill we felt. The food was not good. I remember burnt porridge for breakfast, and soup in chipped enamel mugs at supper time, when we also had little round biscuits. We put these in the soup and saw them swell to twice their size, and felt that we were getting more in that way.

Unless we were very ill we had to get out of bed and kneel to say our prayers each night under the watchful eyes of Miss Ray. I remember once when I first went to the cottage and was told to say my prayers I knelt on one knee beside my bed, with my bent elbow resting on the bed and my face in my hand as I prayed. Can you picture it? Miss Ray shook me harshly and interrupted my prayers, telling me that I was a naughty girl to pray in such an irreverent position. To this I replied, 'But Father does it!', and was told not to be impertinent! But Daddy *did* used to kneel like that when I was a little girl and he was praying with us. He knelt on his left knee with his right elbow resting on his right knee and his right hand over his eyes, and his left arm encircling me as I knelt beside him. How I missed him, and how I cried that night at the cottage.

To pass the time when we were ill in bed there were jig-saws that we could do. I remember one French puzzle of 1000 pieces with a picture of a grapevine full of grapes. I could not possibly tackle it, but Dorothy mastered it one time that we were at the cottage together. We also sewed canvas work and did some knitting. Reading was confined to a whole library full of twopenny paperbacks with such titles as *Jessica's First Prayer,* *Christy's Old Organ, A Peep Behind The Scenes* and *Teddy's Button.* There was one called *Misunderstood,*' but Miss Hare did not approve of that one as she thought that we might identify with Humphrey, the child that felt he was misunderstood. There were some books for older readers in the cottage 'library', but never enough to satisfy avid readers like Dorothy.

On Sundays we had to read periodicals like *The Baptist Times* and *The British Weekly* and missionary magazines and certain Sunday journals that had Bible searching competitions.

At one time when I was about twelve or thirteen I spent several weeks at the cottage, not because I was really ill but because I had eruptions of spots which would not go away. I was alone for much of the time and I found in a cupboard in my bedroom bundles of the *Boy's Own Paper*, in complete sets. No one suggested that I was allowed to read them, and I took it for granted that they were hidden because they were BOY'S OWN, and I supposed should not be read by GIRLS! I read a whole exciting serial, covering perhaps six months of the publication, standing in the doorway of the cupboard, ready to shut the door and scamper into bed if the nurse should come up. The story was 'In the Heart of the Silent Sea', the adventures of a crew in a balloon who were drifting across the Atlantic and came down in the Sargasso Sea. I also learned that cold baths were good for boys, but I cannot remember anything else that I learned by reading what I took for granted was 'forbidden' literature.

Medical treatment was very basic. Castor oil was administered when it was considered necessary. Salt was put on the spoon and you had to rub your lips and tongue with salt, and hold your nose. Salt was used as a gargle for sore throats, and linseed or bread poultice was applied if a cold went down to your chest.

One time Dorothy and I were found to have nits in our hair when we returned from the holidays. We all had regular hair inspection, and it was suggested that we had picked up the lice in the train as we travelled down from Derby. Maybe we had got them from the children who attended the Gospel Hall Sunday School. Anyway, Dorothy and I were both banished to the cottage for a few days where our hair was washed daily with carbolic soap, and some strong smelling oil was rubbed into the scalp, and we had to live and sleep in rubber bathing caps until the lice had been eradicated. The disgrace was humiliating, but at least we were in it together, and so it didn't seem so bad.

Another time I was at the cottage with Kitty Heberlet. She no longer had the ringlets that she sported when she and I were bridesmaids at Auntie Elsie's wedding. Kitty was a bright child, in the same form as Phyllis. This time, at the cottage, we were talking about heaven and angels and Kitty asserted with utmost conviction that she had once seen an angel beside her playbox in the nursery. I felt very envious of her and sad that I seemed to be shut out from such experiences.

Through the years there were different ladies in charge of the Cottage. There was Miss Reeve, and Nurse Smart (whom we called 'Nursie', which gave an indication of our feelings for her), and Nurse Kay Smith (sister of the novelist Shelia Kay Smith) and during the mid-years of the War there was Nurse Stringer. I remember one night she was with a group of us invalids at the cottage, we were all wrapped in blankets, sitting round the dying embers of a fire in the grate, with the sound of gun-fire and shrapnel falling as a zeppelin raid was going on somewhere in the vicinity. We children were making jokes and singing to keep up our spirits, when Nurse Stringer admonished us sternly and said, 'Prepare to meet thy God!' and reduced us to silence.

Truly, in those early days, the cottage was presided over by strict Victorian, nonconformist Christians.

Miss Hare used to read prayers daily at school, and during the War there was one prayer that she used in which she prayed for our men at the front to give them strength and courage, and to the wounded, hope and comfort, and to the dying, peace, and to the dead, Life Everlasting. On one occasion one of the nurses from the cottage was reading the prayer, when she paused suddenly and stumbled and hurriedly finished the prayer omitting the final sentence. She could not bring herself to utter a prayer for the dead.

9

Home On Furlough – 1911

Nineteen hundred and eleven was the year of the coronation of King George V and Queen Mary, and I remember that we children all had coronation souvenirs, little lockets and brooches with pictures of the King and Queen on them. These have long since been lost, but one vivid memory remains, of the school building illuminated by 'real' fairy lights. They were night lights set in little glass jars of red, white and blue, and placed all along the window-sills both upstairs and downstairs, and along the gutterings of the roof. When these were lit what a sight it was to see the school outlined in little lights that twinkled in the breeze!

Father and Mother came home to England in 1911, bringing Phyllis to school. She was seven in July and so entered as a boarder in September of that year. Eric was only four in October, so not ready for boarding school, and he returned to India with our parents after the end of their leave in October 1911.

Curiously, I remember very little about that year when Mother and Father were with us. I have no actual recollection of their arrival nor a clear picture of their departure at the end of their furlough. It was as if the wrench of their first parting two years before and the knowledge and fear of our inevitable further separation made it impossible for me to appreciate fully their presence while we were together. I don't remember when they came. Dorothy and I certainly did not go to London or to Tilbury to meet them. I suppose they came to Sevenoaks Tubs Hill station, I don't think that we even went to the station to meet the train. They arrived at the school, we were told that they were in the Reception Room, and we went to meet them there. They probably stayed a few nights in the Guest Room on the top storey of the school, and then – who knows? – perhaps went to Derby to visit their relations soon afterwards. That is all that I can suppose from a hazy partial recall.

During their furlough Father did rent a furnished house in Bayham Road, Sevenoaks for some weeks. I remember Phyllis suffered from asthma, and that she and Eric had whooping-cough during that time in Sevenoaks. We used to walk down to the gas works near Bat-and-Ball railway station because the fumes from the gasometers were supposed to act as a cure for whooping-cough! Near that station there was a stretch of water with swans on it and a farm with a lot of pigs, and we called the walk 'Pigs and Swans'. When we went out for our daily 'crocodile' walks from school we used to ask the mistress in charge if we could go down St John's and visit the pigs and swans, but we rarely got our wish. It wasn't considered to be a particularly pretty or interesting walk for a school party even if the smell from the gas works cured whooping-cough.

I don't remember anything about the Bayham Road house either; I suppose I never slept there as I was still a boarder at the school. During the summer holidays Father rented a furnished house for us in Burton Road, Derby, so that he could see as much as possible of all his relations. I remember that, as tenants of that house, we were entitled on payment of five shillings to have a key to a little park, which we entered with a sense of pride of possession and were we played most days with our wooden hoops and skipping-ropes and battledore and shuttlecock. I remember that there was a hoarding with posters on it in the road near our house. One of these showed the head of a zebra and was advertising Zebra grate polish. We children always said 'Good morning Mr Zebra' as we passed him.

We picked wild flowers from the verge beside the road. We had competitions to see how many grasses we could find. I remember Phyllis found a stalk of quaker grass which none of us had in our collections and ever afterwards I felt that 'quivery-quakey' grass belonged to Phyllis. We had Robertson's marmalade, Gold and Silver shred, and decorated the kitchen walls with gollywogs from the jars. Mother made a lentil paste for our supper which she called 'mock crab'. As I had never tasted real crab, and liked this paste spread thickly on bread it really didn't matter what it was called. She also made a special sweet for parties with half a tinned peach placed, hollow side down, on a slice of sponge cake and surrounded by whipped cream which she called 'poached eggs.'

We of course were a teetotal family, though the adults drank hop bitters, a non-alcoholic beer. A man called each week with the hop bitters and also brought a large stone bottle of ginger-beer. Father complained one week that the ginger-beer was flat. The next week when he unscrewed the stopper on the new bottle a jet of ginger-beer shot up to the ceiling, and wasted half the contents of the stone bottle. What little things one remembers for years!

Mother wasn't very well or very happy at that time. I think that she found it was a strain cooking and caring for us all after having servants in India. She did not find it easy to demonstrate her love for us. She was probably dreading the inevitable separation as we all were. Our behaviour wasn't good either, we were disobedient, and we frequently quarrelled among ourselves and had rows with Mother. I remember one temper tantrum that I suffered when Dorothy had to put her strong arms around me and hold me forcibly until I calmed down.

Father was very often away from home on preaching tours for the B.M.S. When we were back in Sevenoaks he preached at the Vine Baptist Chapel which we attended. I was filled with a complicated mixture of pride in the feeling that 'this is my Daddy' and apprehension about what he might say or do. I remember one Sunday evening when he took a service for the whole school and made us learn the words and tune and sing an Oriya hymn.

We three girls had of course spoken Oriya and the exercise was fairly easy for us, and Daisy and Grace and Ivy Long, and Edna Jarry, and Patty and Ivy Grundy would also have known Oriya, but for the daughters of missionaries from other parts of India, and from other countries of the world, 'Bodhu Probhu dharma Rajor Prutwe sumodoya . . .' would be a gibberish of sounds. Of course Father translated it and based his sermon on its message. Anyway, as missionaries' daughters we were all used to missionary fathers preaching to us, and some other people's fathers did much more peculiar things, such as dressing up in the native dress of the people of the lands in which they were working, or imitating the buzz of mosquitoes or the cry of jackals! We had heard it all in our time!

Our school had been opened for the daughters of missionaries in 1838, and there was a companion school for the sons of
missionaries. When I first went to Sevenoaks the boys' school
was at Blackheath. Our Grandpa Pike and his four sons had
been at school there many years ago, and the boys were known,
in fun, as Black Heathens. In 1912 the School for the Sons of
Missionaries moved to Mottingham in Kent, and became
Eltham College.

The majority of our parents worked for two societies, the
Baptist Missionary Society and the London Missionary
Society. There were also some whose parents worked for other
societies which I know as an adult, but they were quite
meaningless to me as a child. There was quite a rivalry between
those belonging to the B.M.S. and the L.M.S. We used to shout
like football supporters about the superiority of our own
society, while we climbed higher and higher on the furniture in
a game of 'Kings of the Castle.' Each month magazines
published by different societies were put out on the dining
tables and we dashed to read them to see if there was any news
of our parents or of those of our friends. When I was young I did
not realise that Father and Mother would never be mentioned
in *News From Afar* though their pictures might appear in
Wonderlands or *The Missionary Herald*. When missionaries were
coming home on furlough their portraits might be printed in
the Society's periodical telling of their arrival in this country
and again on their departure back to the Mission field. When
this referred to any of our parents we would sing 'Eternal
Father strong to save . . .' during prayers or Sunday evening
hymn singing. There might also be news of special events, or of
transfers to different stations, and of births and deaths. About
that time the Long children, Daisy, Grace and Ivy, heard the
tragic news of the death of their Father. In 1911 there would
have appeared in the *Missionary Herald* the news of the furlough
of the Rev. Gordon S. and Mrs Wilkins, with perhaps a
photograph of them and their two little children, and now there
would be news of their departure with their little son in
October.

Eric had a congenital weakness of the muscles of one eye
which caused it to squint. This was corrected by spectacles
which he had just before his fourth birthday. He was now going
to be 'an only child' in Russelkhonda where Father was to be

Eric Gordon aged 4, in Russelkhonda

stationed when he returned to India, and to compensate slightly Father bought him a much more expensive present than any of us had ever had. We did not grudge it to him, but we envied him still being with Mother and Father. The present was a large toy motor-car, big enough for him to pedal about in, and I hope to amuse himself in his lonely childhood in an up-country station in India where there were no other English children for him to play with. There is a glossy photograph of him taken sitting in his little car. Poor little chap! He looks very solemn in his new glasses, but at least he was going to be with Mother and Father while we three girls were left in England. There were two incidents that I remember in connection with saying 'goodbye' to Mother in October 1911. We Lower School children did not go to church on Sunday evenings but had hymn singing in the schoolroom, and I chose 'God be with you till we meet again' to be sung on the last Sunday before they left. Mother was with us at the hymn singing and she protested rather feebly, 'We don't want to sing that, do we?' and I think that the mistress who was playing the piano tried to put me off too, but I insisted that we should sing it. After all, what could be more appropriate? The hymn must have been written for just such an occasion, and I didn't see why we shouldn't sing it. I don't know where Father was that evening, probably preaching a farewell sermon at the Baptist Church, but Mother had to try to sing in spite of the upsurge of her emotions, and I sang loudly, 'God be with you till we meet again . . . till we me . . . ee . . . eet, till we meet at Jesu's feet. . . .'

That night Mother came up to give me a bath and see me to bed, and while she was cutting my toenails I said, 'This is the last time in my life that you'll ever cut my toenails.'

Mother protested but I said, 'No, I shall be twelve when I see you again and I shall be too old to have my toenails cut by you then.' I was hardened to the fact of the separation.

So one day in October 1911 Mother and Father and Eric left England to return to India. I think they must have gone by train to Dover and crossed the Channel, and then taken a train to Marseilles, and boarded the steamer there. I don't know the name of the ship on which they sailed on that occasion, but I remember we used to chant, 'Ma sails from Marseilles on Thursday . . .' thinking it was a very funny joke. It might have been this time of her departure that we chanted this song, or

71

perhaps it was 1915 when she returned after bringing Eric to school. I don't know.

At the end of this furlough there is a letter from Dorothy, dated October 1911 to:

'My dearest Mother, Father and Eric.
I have got the telegram, thank you so much for sending it. I wonder if it was stormy going across. I shall be glad when the sea journey is over and you are safe in India, although you are so far from us in India, I feel you are safer than when on the sea. I feel I *must* write to you so as I have finished all my study I am writing. It seems such a long time since this morning. I am trying hard to be brave and so are Joyce and Phyllis, but it is very difficult as the tears *will* come, but thats enough about that I shall be making you sad if I talk like this. I know we shall all meet again so must be cheerful and wait mustn't I?. . . .'

We had to wait many years before we saw Father again, and four years before Mother and Eric returned. When Eric went to Eltham College in 1915 we saw him sometimes in term time. It was always a great occasion when brothers from Eltham came over to spend a day with their sisters in Sevenoaks. We all enjoyed the boys' visits, but when in exchange their sisters were invited over to see their brothers we three could now join the party, as we too had a brother at Eltham College SSM. We rarely saw Eric during the holidays and we hardly knew him as we had been separated for so long. The poor boy was very shy, but our day spent in the boys' school was a highlight in the term! Among the boys who were at school with my brother was the son of a missionary in China, Eric Liddell, who became an Olympic runner.

10

We Three Sisters

Phyllis was the baby of the school when she came to W.H. in 1911, but Joan Brown, who was older than Phyllis, was always spoken of by Miss Hare and the mistresses as the 'school baby.' We resented this! Joan was the smaller of the two, with a round face and curly hair, Phyllis was a fair little girl, tall for her age and rather solemn and quiet. The big girls tended to make a fuss of the school baby, but I don't remember Phyllis getting that 'spoiling'. She soon made friends with the children of her own age, and all through her school-days she had a group of close friends, many of whom remained her friends for years. When she was about eleven or twelve one of her closest friends, Beth Piper, died and she felt her loss very keenly. Dorothy was not only her oldest sister and her 'school mother' but she became her comforter, adviser and friend, and a substitute for Mother. Phyllis and I were always friends, and we did many things together, and I was admitted, so to speak, on the outside of her intimate circle of friends.

Miss Hare frowned upon close relationships between two girls, and would try to separate any two who were seen walking hand-in-hand, or with their arms round each other and heads close as they exchanged whispered confidences. This was considered to be 'unhealthy', as was also what we called 'having a pash on' older girls or a mistress. Phyllis had a close relationship with a member of the staff, and many a younger girls had 'a pash' on her when she was a prefect and later Head Girl. She was capable of giving and receiving love and many benefited from her friendship. She usually had two 'special friends' so that her circle consisted of three, and this was never disapproved of or broken up by those in authority.

Phyllis was a very clever little girl, and school work came

easily to her. She was soon found to be doing work that was too easy for her in the class in which she was entered, and she was moved up to a higher form. This meant that she was only one year behind me, though there was a two and a half years difference in our ages. She could read and write well, had no difficulty in spelling correctly, and had we had places in class would certainly always have been top of the form. Miss Hare did not approve of a competitive spirit in the class and so we were always placed alphabetically and never allowed to know who was top and who was bottom. Our marks were given in grades and we knew if we were in Grade I, II or III, or in IV which was a failure, but did not know who was first, second or third.

Phyllis was very musical, and made rapid progress in learning to play the piano, and later also with the violin. She used to play piano and violin solos in the school concerts, and I would listen with pride – and with envy – as she performed.

Later when I was old enough to learn solo singing she would play my accompaniment, and give me support and encouragement. I also used to give recitations with musical accompaniment – notably 'High Tide off the Coast of Lincolnshire' (when, Mary went to call the cattle home') – and Phyllis played, with spirit and the necessary sympathetic understanding, the descriptive music that was written to accompany the speaker. We used to hold impromptu and amusing private sessions together when I would recite a poem or invent a story which I would declaim while Phyllis improvised a musical accompaniment to it much as a cinema organist performed in the days of the silent films. We had great fun together over this. Phyllis also had a party piece which she would perform on occasion. She would sit with her back to the piano, and crossing her hands behind her back would play a piece of music in this position, much to the amusement of those who watched and listened.

When she first came to school we did many things together. We shared a garden, a plot about ten feet by five, surrounded by a stone curb, in which we sowed packets of annual flower seeds, sweet peas at the top, virginian stock round the edges, and clarkia and love-in-mist and forget-me-nots. The seed merchants, Ryders and also Suttons, sent seed catalogues to each of us children personally, and we chose penny packets of

74

this, and perhaps a twopenny packet of something else, and sent our postal order for ninepence or a shilling, and received our little parcels back amidst great excitement – and hope. Unfortunately it took us some time and much disappointment before we realized that with HA on the packet the seeds would grow in our garden, but that HHA would not grow from seed out in the open, and that some seeds labelled P and BA might not flower until next year. In 1915, the summer that Mother returned to England bringing Eric to school, we planned our garden to be all in mauve and white because we believed that these colours would please her best.

But in our younger days our garden held another mystery and secret for us. Under the bushes at the top of the garden we buried a doll in a tin box with a lid, and we used to sprinkle the shrine with 'holy' water, and wish on it. We did this also once when we were on holiday at our Uncle's farm at Sawley Grange. Here we dug a hole in the field, lined it with clay, and made a lid of woven twigs over the box with the doll in it. This lid we covered with turf, and then used it as a 'holy' place at which we wished. At one time we wished to find a penny under our pillow each morning, and getting our cousin to put it there each night we 'discovered' the penny with great pleasure and excitement in the morning! When we opened the tin box later we found that there were spiders and 'creepy-crawlies' in with the doll, and so we rescued her from her grave.

Phyllis and I also had a 'house' together up on the bank under the pine trees that grew round the area known as the 'Frying-pan' in the school grounds. Here we cut steps up to our house, defined the area of the rooms with stones, made a 'kitchen' with a fireplace and 'sink'. This latter was a tin box with a hole in it which was stopped by a cork. We made a drain leading from it down the slope, and when we had 'washed up' in the sink, we let the water out and it ran – most satisfactorily – down the drain. We made mud pies which we decorated with flower petals and leaves and seeds and called these 'cakes', and sometimes made them in two or three tiers, and offered them to members of the staff as 'wedding cakes'. We brewed teas from small unripe horse chestnuts, but warned people who were offered a cup that they mustn't really drink it. We played 'house' for many hours, I am not sure but it must have been for more than one summer term. We had a lot of free time to spend in the garden as, in those days, we had no lessons in the afternoons, and were too young to be playing tennis or netball.

We also had free time every Sunday afternoon when we spent the hours from two to four in our own rooms, writing letters, painting or reading. Sisters were allowed to be together and Dorothy, Phyllis and I spent a couple of hours in one bedroom each Sunday afternoon, which made up for not seeing each other much during the week.

On Saturdays we were allowed access to the sweets that we brought back to school at the beginning of term. These were labelled with our name and stored in the cupboard which was opened once a week for us to choose what we wanted from our store. Many of us tried to make this store last out the whole term. Sometimes we received a box of chocolates or tin of sweets for our birthday, or as a present from the relations with whom we stayed for the holidays. On half-term holidays we were allowed to buy sweets – four pennyworth each or later six pennyworth. The order was given to the prefects who were commissioned to go to the shop and purchase our require-ments. Poor shopkeeper, having to weigh out ten or more separate ounces of this or that particular sweet! It was a long time before I realized that you couldn't have just one pennyworth of sweets that cost more than 4d. a quarter! But then those were the days when a bar of Sharpes Creamy Toffee cost a halfpenny, and you could buy a halfpennyworth of sherbert, or a liquorice lace for the same sum. When we had sweets we always shared them with our sisters. If I were unexpectedly given some sweets, or an apple, or some other luxury like a piece of cake, I would seek out Dorothy or Phyllis – or both – to share it with them, and they would do the same.

We sisters were very fond of each other, and I don't remember that we ever quarrelled – seriously – when we were at school.

From time to time we were allowed to keep pets at school, and then if they died or became a nuisance there would be an order banning any more. Phyllis and I had rabbits and white mice, and of course each year a batch of silkworms, and we also rescued fledgling birds that we tried to rear. Dorothy went in for more exotic creatures, a grass snake from Gamages, a red squirrel, kept in the greenhouse, and then a jerboa (a kangaroo rat from Africa). When tragedy struck these she contented

The three sisters at school in 1913

herself with ordinary white rats, but she always, all her life, was devoted to animals and was surrounded by them.

Phyllis and I depended on Dorothy for comfort when we were lonely or miserable, and we turned to her for advice and help when we needed them. She suffered just as much as we did on account of the separation from our parents, but she was much braver at facing it. She felt responsibility as the eldest, and shouldered it with courage. She didn't find school work as easy as Phyllis did, but she tackled it with determination with her sights always set on becoming a doctor. This she became after years of work and effort. Although she was able to play the piano better than I could, she realized her limitations and gave up having lessons. She was always acutely aware of Father's financial situation (she used to explain to us 'We are as poor as chapel mice, who are even poorer than church mice') and did her best to save our parents' money and never ask for things they couldn't afford to give us.

None of us was particularly good at games, but Dorothy played a very plucky game of hockey and was in the first eleven, and she enjoyed hockey matches in spite of all the bruises she received. She played tennis with a very strong underarm serve with a spin on it, which gave her a place in the school six. Ladies had hardly started to serve overarm at the time that Dorothy was learning to play tennis before the First World War. Our cousin Elsie taught Phyllis and me to serve overarm from the age of twelve, and we both played in the school's first three couples, but we never got the pace or spin on our service that Dorothy achieved underarm.

Phyllis and I also played netball and, mostly because of the advantage of our height, both played in school teams. I was not allowed to play hockey for some time – I was not considered to be strong enough in health – and so never played very much. I don't remember Phyllis talking much about hockey, or expressing much enjoyment in the game, but she probably played regularly.

Dorothy went through a rebellious period during adolescence and used to say that she was Cain 'with her hand against every man', and I think that she was often in trouble with authority, but as a young sister I was not allowed to know much about this. I remember once that I found her reading a book by Mrs Henry Wood which had been banned by Miss Hare (I don't know why) and when I said innocently, 'I thought you were not allowed to read that!' she snapped at me and told me to mind my own business. Dorothy, who had difficulty in learning to read as a small child, was now an avid reader and was hardly ever to be found without a book in her hands. She also went through a period of activity when she was trying to write a million strokes! Having been told that it would be impossible for anyone to write a million strokes she set out to prove that she could do it. She filled sheet after sheet of rough note books with pages covered with strokes. They were in bundles of five, four strokes down with one crossing them out, making a group of five which was easy to count. I don't know for how many days she continued with the project or how many thousands of strokes that she made, or whether she ever got to the million, but I know that she had a good try!

Dorothy was also very skilful at playing Diabolo (a two-headed top worked on a string tied to two sticks). Constant practice made her the school champion. She was artistic, good at drawing and embroidery and did crochet work. I remember her working on a wide border of lace for a tablecloth for

Mother. We were 'dressed by the school' and had a uniform, but Dorothy had her own ideas about dress. Once she went into Sevenoaks determined to buy an 'old gold' ribbon for the sash of her cream 'Summer-Sunday' dress. The shopkeeper hadn't a ribbon of any such colour, and, much to Dorothy's disgust, tried to persuade her to buy a 'pretty pink' or a 'nice blue' instead! Her heart was set on 'old gold'.

Dorothy had her own close friends, and in adolescence had a 'crush' on one of the mistresses. I remember that she used to pick bunches of wild flowers, and do elaborate arrangements of them in unusual containers to present as an offering to her beloved. In her last few years at school she developed close friendships with two younger mistresses who were not many years older than she was, and these friendships lasted for the rest of their lives.

I myself never seemed to be able to make and keep friends at school. I tried hard, and befriended new girls when they came, but as soon as they had settled down they found and made their own friends – and I was left alone. I tried hard to have a 'pash' on one of the mistresses too as Dorothy and Phyllis each had a beloved, but somehow it wouldn't come! I was too self-centred, too taken up with my own problems and anxieties to be able to love anyone other than my two sisters.

11

Clothes

I was at school at Walthamstow Hall for twelve years. My first
term, when I was six and my parents were in Sevenoaks, I was
a day-girl, but when I was seven and until I was eighteen I was
a boarder. When I first entered the school it was known as a
'Home and School for the Daughters of Missionaries', and the
parents of all the girls were serving on the mission field, and we
were all boarders. This changed as the years went by. First,
day-girls were admitted from Sevenoaks and the district
around, and then, as the school grew, girls came to the
boarding school even though their parents were not missionaries.

When I first came to the school there was no general uniform
worn by all the girls, but a few of us were 'dressed by the
school'. This meant that we wore the same pattern of clothes as
each other. We were not exactly 'charity children' as our
parents paid for our clothes, but it showed everyone that we
had no guardian who would undertake the responsibility of
looking after us, and so the school provided all that we needed
and charged the account to our parents. We three were not very
happy with this arrangement and we felt rather like 'orphans'
when some of the other girls were wearing pretty frocks which
had been bought for them by their grandma or auntie. In later
years when day-girls were admitted to the school and there
were some boarders who were not from missionary families it
was decided to adopt a school uniform, and then all of us were
dressed alike.

During the first few years that I was at school the building
was very cold in the winter and we all suffered from chilblains.
There were open coal fires in the classrooms, and some hot
water pipes in the corridors upstairs, but the passages and

cloakrooms were very cold, and we had to go along a passageway open to the wind and rain on our way to the gym. Most of us had been born in warmer climates and we felt the cold, in spite of the layers of woollies that we were made to wear. First of all there were long-sleeved combinations, and, I believe, a long-sleeved vest as well, a liberty bodice, woollen bloomers with linings, flannel petticoats, black woollen stockings, a serge frock and 'hug-me-tight' or 'monkey-jacket'. When we were young we wore a blue overall over all this in the mornings, and a starched white pinafore in the afternoons. This pinny had frills round the neck and armholes which were often very stiff with starch and gauffered so that it tickled our ears! We were given a clean pinny on Wednesday afternoons and on Sundays. Our serge frocks had high necks, which were finished by white 'tuckers' which had to be sewn in. As we grew older the high necks of the frocks had bones in them to keep them upright. We wore black buttoned boots. Our hats were made of hard felt in the winter (though Phyllis at one time had a black 'beaver' hat. I remember that it was furry, though whether it was real beaver fur or not I don't know.)

In summer we wore hard straw hats, the 'straw bashers' seen in illustrations to girls school stories of the period. On Sundays these hats had a white ribbon band, while our weekday ones had the school colours of orange and black. The hats were kept on by an elastic under the chin which left a red mark on our necks while the stiff straw hat left a red mark on our foreheads. On Sundays in the summer we wore white wincey frocks on which we had pink or blue sashes. Dorothy's 'old gold' ribbon, would not have been allowed.

Our hair was left to grow long and was usually plaited, and tied with a black ribbon, or a white one on Sundays. The older girls wore a wide black bow at the nape of the neck, with sometimes another black bow at the end of the plait. None but the very young had her hair cut short. When I was fourteen years of age the 'bob' came into fashion and I had my long and rather straggling hair cut off to an almost shoulder-length 'bob'. This aroused a good deal of criticism from old-fashioned adults, but when young women in the First World War found that long hair was inconvenient in their active wartime lives, the 'bob' led to the more shapely and attractive 'shingle' and sometimes to a short, boyish 'Eton crop', and I continued to wear my hair cut short.

When school uniform was introduced we wore gym tunics in the mornings and blouses and skirts in the afternoons. The gym tunics were first made of heavy serge for the winter and alpaca for the summer. They were of navy blue at first, but during the First World War there was a shortage of navy blue dye (I believed that the secret formula for 'Prussian blue dye' was really held in Prussia) and the school uniform was changed to 'nigger brown'. When we were first measured for our gym tunics we were required to kneel down and the tape measure was taken to the ground. As the years went by the fashion dictated that the tunics became shorter and shorter until in the end they were well above the knee. At first we wore black woollen stockings with our navy tunics and navy blue bloomers almost down to our knees, but later we were required to wear very long brown cotton stockings and short, neat brown panties. We wore a webbing sash with the tunic, tied in a neat sailor's knot. Some girls looked very smart in their gym tunics. I was not one of them, I was too tall and ungainly.

We wore school uniform all during the week, but on Sunday afternoons and sometimes on Wednesday evenings were allowed a break form strict uniform. I remember that I had a gorgeous wide piece of hair-ribbon which was bright red, satin on one side and shot silk on the other, and with what a thrill I tied it in a huge bow on my hair on Wednesday evenings! How I loved it! I was always trying to be a bit different from other people. I remember that I had a black felt winter hat one year and I sewed the gorgeous 'eye' of a peacock's feather on to the ribbon in the front. I expect I was made to take it off! One summer when I was staying for the holidays with Auntie Alice there was a cream straw hat with a wreath of artificial nasturtiums round it in a shop window. It was 'sale price', end of season, only 7/6, and I gazed at it daily and longed to buy it, but had not the money, and really knew that I would never have any occasion to wear it. Oh how I dreamed of that hat!

When I was about sixteen I was given a dress allowance of £12 a year and expected to buy all my clothes for that sum. I remember that one of the first things I bought was a black shiny raincoat, and longed for a rainy day so that I could wear it. Later I bought a grey velvet frock (which can be seen in a

82

family photograph taken to celebrate Mother and Father's Silver Wedding). I loved wearing that frock, which was not school uniform, and also on Sundays and special occasions to dress in a cream frock decorated with white beads which I wore with grey silk stockings and grey suede shoes. I used to put these shoes and stockings on when I was getting undressed at night, and place a mirror on the floor with a lighted candle beside it, and admire the beauty of my grey clad feet in secret! So my footwear during my schooldays had changed from long black buttoned boots to pale grey suede court shoes! I remember that once in my early youth I had attended a Christmas party at Auntie Annie's house in Derby, and I had worn my boots throughout the evening, quite forgetting that I had brought a pair of slippers that I was supposed to change into when I arrived. I found them in the bedroom when it was time to go home, and I was heartily scolded for my thoughtlessness. Now I was only too anxious to wear pretty shoes, and wore them even in the privacy of my bedroom.

12

The Headmistress

Miss Hare was Headmistress of Walthamstow Hall for twenty years and so was there throughout the twelve years that I was at school. I think her full name was Sophia Louisa Hare but have not seen that in writing. She signed all our reports and her letters to parents as 'Sophie Hare', we children of course changed that to 'Soapy Hair' and thought that a very funny joke. Not that we would ever let this be heard by Miss Hare herself. Miss K. Little we called 'The Kettle', and she knew it, and shared the joke with us. But Miss Hare was different. She was a figure of authority and we were very much in awe of her. Many of the girls developed a great affection for her as they grew older and got to know her well. It was said that Dorothy was devoted to her, but I'm not sure this was so. Phyllis of course ended up as Head Girl in Miss Hare's last year at the school and during that year she must have been in close contact with her.

For me Miss Hare was always the figure of authority, stern and awe-inspiring, never a person in whom I could confide. Though I have heard a story told of how, when I was a small child and new in the school, Miss Hare caught me running down the corridor (a thing that was strictly forbidden) and when she stopped me I flung my arms around her and kissed her! She told this story to other people and left me feeling silly and embarrassed. But we did kiss Miss Hare very frequently and were kissed by her. At least once a week (it couldn't have been every night could it?) we lined up in a formal order to have a word with her and to be kissed 'goodnight', or if there were a number of cases of 'flu or measles or other illness about, we would solemnly shake hands with her and wish her 'good-night'. When other mistresses were on duty they were not expected to kiss us or be kissed by us, it was always a formal handshake then, only Miss Hare attempted to take the place of Mother with a goodnight kiss. It was a wonderfully kind gesture on her part, an attempt to create an atmosphere of home, and to give her an opportunity to speak to each child, but it must have been an ordeal for her, as it actually was for us, especially if we were in trouble and undergoing punishment. I remember one amusing incident during the War when we were rather hungry. One girl had stolen more than her fair share of biscuits and stuffed them up the leg of her knickers. As she kissed Miss Hare goodnight the elastic broke and the biscuits came tumbling out on the floor!

We were given a half-day's holiday each year on Miss Hare's birthday. When we were very young we would ask her how old she was, to which she would give the grown-up's reply, 'As old as my tongue and a little older than my teeth.' When we were discussing this later among ourselves it is reported that I was heard to say, with great conviction, when somebody wondered if she could be a hundred, 'Oh no, she's not a day more than ninety!' This remark was of course repeated with laughter at my expense.

Our Miss Hare had two sisters, Miss Ethel and Miss Mary Hare who ran a school for deaf boys and girls. They were pioneers in teaching the deaf to communicate with hearing people without relying entirely on sign language. In those early years before the First World War, deaf-mutes (as they were called) were often left untutored and unable to communicate with others, so that they appeared to be 'village idiots'. The pioneering work in educating the deaf done by the two Miss Hares was widely recognized, and when they retired there was a school established in London which bore the name of the Mary Hare School for the Deaf. Sometimes the sisters brought a number of their brighter children down to Sevenoaks to mix with us for a day. We had some difficulty in understanding their speech which was uttered in strange tones of voice and with exaggerated articulation, but gradually we were able to understand each other as the deaf lip-read what we were saying and we learned to interpret the noises that they made. We also learned finger spelling to talk to them, though this was not encouraged as they were supposed to use their voices. I enjoyed the deaf children's visits, and found them very interesting, and they played a part in turning me later to choose speech therapy as a career.

I think that Miss Hare had some brothers, but whether they were the Adolphus Hare and Augustus Hare whose names we heard mentioned at times I don't know. We never knew of a brother coming to visit Miss Hare at school, and never saw or heard of any nephews or nieces so perhaps none of her family married. She was very lonely in her old age. She showed great affection for small children, and she would make a fuss of the youngest girls in the kindergarten. She was very distressed when Mildred Marshall, the school baby, died and she had a photograph of her in her sitting-room for years. And then there was Lena Morgan too. She was very young when she died, soon after I went to the school.

Miss Hare was a very handsome woman, slight and upright, and gave the impression of being very tall. She had a straight nose and a beautiful profile, and piercing brown eyes. When in later years she wore pince-nez her stern gaze was even more frightening. She always dressed beautifully, and when her hair went white she had it Marcel waved and she looked very regal.

She had been educated at the North London Collegiate School under the headship of Miss Buss who followed the same lines of teaching as Miss Beale, the Principal of Cheltenham Ladies' College. These are the ladies of whom we said:

> 'Miss Buss and Miss Beale
> They do not feel.
> Miss Beale and Miss Buss
> They are not like us.'

I am sure that Miss Hare did feel, but she didn't approve of showing her feelings, nor of any of us showing signs of 'sentimentality' which she was always condemning.

But she tried to make us feel that, in the words of our early School Song which we sang with gusto to the tune of Bonnie Dundee:

> 'Our school is our home we are all proud to say,
> For our parents are missionaries far, far away.
> From the East to the West, from the North to the South,
> The praise o our school is in everyone's mouth!

So up with our Colours, the Orange and Black,
We'll shout for our School 'till our voice echoes back!
Girls, Teachers and Old Girls, oh do let us all
Give a hip! hip! hurrah; for Walthamstow Hall!

When Miss Hare was appointed to be Principal in 1901 the school was under the influence of the rigid puritan discipline of the late Victorian era. Miss Unwin was Principal in my mother's time, and she had often told us of the strict upbringing she had had under her. One of the major changes that Miss Hare made was to the timetable. We still had to learn by heart passages of Scripture each day, but we had fewer lessons and more free time. We only had lessons in the mornings, the afternoons were given up to games and walks. On Wednesdays and Saturdays we had long afternoons in the open air, and no lessons in the evenings. On other days we had a couple of lessons after tea, and then from six o'clock onwards time for prep, before supper and bed. Also there was time for letter writing, our weekly letter to our parents.

On Wednesday evenings we would gather in Miss Hare's room and she would read aloud to us. During the War we were expected to be sewing or knitting while we sat on the floor listening to her beautiful voice reading, and Miss Hare would be knitting while she read. Only when she came to an intricate part of her knitting, such as turning the heel of a sock, would she put her knitting down, but she never faltered in her reading. She had a large personal library in her sitting-room and when the senior girls had exhausted all that the Lower School and Upper School libraries had to offer them, Miss Hare would recommend some of her own books, and lend them to the favoured few. Dorothy was an avid reader and so was Phyllis (who later read English at Oxford) and they both were allowed to borrow books from Miss Hare. I was never a great reader, I read slowly and with great difficulty, and so was never offered the loan of any of her books.

In fact my spelling was so bad that Miss Hare held me up to ridicule in front of the whole of the Upper School on one mortifying occasion that I remember. Miss Hare taught some subjects during the week, notably Scripture and current events. Her classes were large, consisting of two or three forms of the Upper School. This day I remember Miss Hare, returning some essays that we had to write for her, announced with great scorn that one girl, JOYCE WILKINS, has spelt the word 'through' as 'threw' and she is what? Fifteen? At that age she should know better. I was sunk in shame! Miss Hare's teaching sessions were so terrifying for me that I don't remember anything she said! Scripture consisted of the history of Judas Maccabe and the Maccabees, and current events was 'History in the Making'. During the First World War we made scrapbooks of newspaper cuttings, and wrote our comments on what we read in note books labelled HITM. Little did Miss Hare realize with what terror I sat through her classes, fearing that I would be held up to ridicule for my ignorance and stupidity, and in consequence not taking in a word of what she was saying!

I remember one day Miss Hare took me to London to the oculist, Mr McLehose, in Harley Street. I wore glasses from about the age of twelve till I was sixteen. These steel-rimmed spectacles were shiny at first but the rims soon turned black, and I found them very disfiguring. I suppose at this time Miss Hare was just finding the long sight of old age coming on, and was consulting Mr McLehose for herself. I remember that his front door in Harley Street was painted bright red. I had had drops in my eyes in preparation for the visit and my vision was blurred, and I couldn't see to read.

After our appointment was over we went to Trafalgar Square and Miss Hare showed me the Standard Yard Measure in brass set into the pavement, and she bought me a facsimile of a newspaper recording the events of a century before. I regret that I soon lost the paper. Because we bought it in Trafalgar Square I always thought that it commemorated the Battle of Trafalgar, but now I think it must have been in 1915 and so was commemorating the Battle of Waterloo of 1815.

After that Miss Hare took me to a restaurant for lunch, and I chose whiting, which I had never had before, and as Alice in Wonderland knew it would, it had its tail in its mouth! I couldn't see properly, and it was full of bones, and I got it all in a terrible mess. What an ordeal! I expect it was rather an ordeal for Miss Hare too. She was very happy dealing with small children, and also with the older girls with whom she could talk intelligently, but I was tongue-tied and too frightened and stupid to respond to her kindness.

Miss Hare was a Christian, otherwise she would not have been appointed Principal of our school, but I do not know to which church she belonged, she attended the different churches from time to time. She conducted prayers daily with the whole school, and talked to us seriously on spiritual matters, and read books such as *The Other Wise Man* to us, and let us sing hymns like:

Gather us in, thou love that fillest all,
Gather our rival faiths within thy fold.
Rend each man's temple-veil and bid it fall,
That we may know that thou hast been of old:
    Gather us in.

We had the idea that perhaps she was a Theosophist. I believe that at one time she was at odds with the strict members of the Board of Governors who ran the school because of her unorthodox views. It was 1913 when I was eleven that rumours started that Miss Hare might be leaving us. I didn't understand what was happening but I knew that she had to go up to London to be interviewed by a committee and we all went about whispering dark hints and fears as to what was going on. And then a telegram came from Miss Hare from London which said 'Put up the flag!', and I knew that that meant that she was staying on. We hoisted the Union Jack and the school flag on the flagstaff, and decorated the front gates with Chinese lanterns and a large WELCOME sign, and the front door with the school motto and lanterns. The Sixth Form girls went down to the station to meet her off the train, one returned in advance to tell us that she was coming, and we lined up on either side of the drive and cheered her as she came. I remember that there was some talk among the big girls that we should take the horse out of the shafts and drag the cab through the gates ourselves, but we didn't actually do that; we rang the bells and cheered and shouted – and we were given a weekend holiday to celebrate. It must have made Miss Hare very happy. She was so obviously loved by so many people, and we were all very glad that she was not leaving us. I was relieved too and carried away in the general excitement, but I was still very much in awe of her.

13

Holidays

Like all small children when the school term was coming to an end we looked forward eagerly to the holidays. We danced about and chanted age-old ditties like:

> 'This time next week where shall I be?
> Not in this academee. . .'

and even, in imitation of boys' public schools:

> 'No more Latin, no more Greek,
> No more of the Prefects' cheek. . .'

adding all kinds of improvised rude lines. But when the holidays actually came they did not always bring us such joy – though of course there were many times when we were very happy. The trouble was that we were very often separated from each other during the holidays, and then we could be very lonely. We had no place that was home to us when we were not at school. How we envied some of the other girls, such as Winifred Wareham who always went to stay with her Grandma on her holidays, and counted that as her home while her parents were abroad. She even belonged to a Guide company during the holidays, and kept her Guide uniform at her home at Granny's.

Uncle George, Father's oldest brother was our legal guardian, but his wife Auntie Annie wasn't eager to look after Gordon's children. Father was fifteen years younger than his brother George, who had three beautiful and talented daughters and a son – all grown up when we knew them. Auntie Annie resented the fact that the penniless younger brother Gordon was able to have a boarding-school education for his daughters which had not been available for hers. She did have us to stay with them in Derby sometimes, but did nothing to entertain us, or even to make sure that we were happily occupied when we were there. She had a marvellous maid, Edith, who had her meals in the kitchen, being provided with inferior butter and cheaper tea than was served in the dining-room. We spent much of our time with Edith who showed us all the affection that we received in that house, though Uncle was quite genial when we met. His little blue-eyed grand-daughter Betty was really the light of his life.

There were two attic bedrooms in the Uttoxeter Road house in Derby; Edith slept in one, and Dorothy and I shared the other. The house was lit by gas in my young days, with incandescent mantles on the flames downstairs, but with batswing jets in the bedroom. We were frightened in that cold dark attic when we had to turn the gas out and jump into bed in the dark, and we often sat at the head of the stairs, listening to the sounds downstairs, and to the trams that rattled past the house, and waiting until we heard Edith coming upstairs to bed before we made that leap in the dark and huddled up under the bedclothes.

While we were still young the house was converted to electricity, and quite unaware of the danger, little Phyllis pushed a pair of silver sugar tongs into the two unprotected holes in the wall plug – and received a shock that threw her across the room. The tongs were distorted into a molten mass.

After Phyllis came to school she and Dorothy often stayed with one uncle and aunt while I was sent to stay with another. Auntie Alice and her husband Uncle Harry had one daughter, Marjorie. They more or less adopted me and I very often spent my holidays with them. Auntie Alice was full of fun and ready to plan entertainment for me. She often took me to the pictures, or to have tea in a café where we ate cream cakes or some other luxury. Uncle Harry was a vegetarian, and careful with money. He worked in his allotment most of the time, and kept chickens, and boiled up earthworms with kitchen scraps to feed them. He was kind to me, but he *would* put his not-too-clean hands each side of my face and kiss me, and he had a dewdrop on the end of his nose and his beard was scrubby. But I remember once I leaned too far over the bannister in his house, and fell over

91

SMACK! into the hall below, and he was the first to pick me up and croon over me and comfort me. It was a wonder that I was not injured in that fall.

I remember too that I had to earn threepence a week pocket-money when I stayed with Auntie Alice and Uncle Harry by cleaning the brass taps in the bathroom and kitchen, and polishing the brass plate on the knocker on the front door, and washing the front doorstep each morning. They kept no maid. As it was usually winter time (I often spent my Christmas holidays with them) my fingers were white and aching with the cold. But Auntie and I used to do amusing things like putting saucers of milk out on the window-sill and then eating the ice with sugar on it. One thing I didn't enjoy when staying with them was that they were keen whist and solo-whist players and needed me to 'make up a four' for their games every evening. I was bored, I hated cards with a 'Hush! this is WHIST' atmosphere.

Uncle and Auntie were always selling their house and buying another, and I never knew what their address would be for the next holiday. Uncle had no fixed job, I think his buying and selling of houses was in the hope of making some money in the transaction. I don't know if he succeeded. There was certainly no sign of money to spare in that household, and his houses were small, much smaller than Uncle George's. I believe that he and Auntie had seventeen homes in their married life.

The place in which we were happiest was of course Uncle Tom's and Auntie Elsie's farm at Sawley Grange. Here our cousin Elsie who worked hard as a farmer's daughter was always ready to teach us how to play tennis, to let us ride her horse Topsy, and to learn to ride her bicycle, to go out in the pony-trap with the milk, to let us feed the calves, and the chickens, look for the eggs (free range), play with the kittens, and wander about the fields with the sheep-dogs. When we were all three together at the farm it was utter bliss, but more often Dorothy and Phyllis were there while I was with Auntie Alice in Long Eaton, and I would only be invited over for the day. But I spent many, many happy hours at Sawley Grange. As well as their daughter Elsie, Uncle and Auntie had three sons, Joe, Frank and Rupert, and when the Great War started all three enlisted, many of their horses were commandeered, and the farm hands were called up and Uncle and Auntie retired to Corner Croft, a house they had built in Sawley village.

Eric, when he came home to school, had very dull and unhappy holidays. He used to stay with Mother's brother, Uncle John Pike, and his wife Auntie Nancy in Derby. They had never had any children and had no idea of how to entertain a small boy. Uncle was very deaf and worked in a printing works all day, and I believe that Eric sometimes spent 'a day at the works' for something to do.

His other holiday home was no better; it was with cousin Mabel Potter and her husband Jim. They had never had any children either, and Jim was a tailor and at work in the shop all day, and Mabel was occupied with 'good works' at the Gospel Hall. By the time Eric had come to England I think that Uncle Tom had retired from Sawley Grange, and gone to live at Corner Croft in Sawley, and so Eric never experienced the joys of our days on the farm.

The four of us had a holiday with Mother in Harrogate in 1915 when Mother brought Eric home to school. There we met Mother's cousin Harold Pike and his wife and their son and daughter. I think their names were Malcolm and Helen. I remember picnics on the moors, and the concert party giving their performances in the open air with their songs and dances and amusing acts. We sang the songs that we heard there for a long time afterwards, and I suppose they were one of the last concert parties and Pierrots and 'Jollity Boys' to be heard. The War called them up. Cousin Harold was killed in the war, and we never met his children again.

Talking of Pierrots reminds me of the Summer of 1909 when Dorothy and I were taken to Llandudno by Auntie Alice and Marjorie, and I remember how we enjoyed the sea and the sands and the donkey rides and the Pierrots in the Happy Valley.

And in 1912 we had a very happy holiday with the Jarrys in Dover. Mrs Jarry's mother and father, the Moodys, ran a commercial hotel (I think it would be called) in Dover, and Dorothy and I had a holiday there with Mr and Mrs Jarry and Edna and Gordon, and we enjoyed ourselves enormously. We learned to call Mr and Mrs Jarry 'Uncle' and 'Auntie' (which annoyed Edna very much, especially if I said 'Uncle Freddie' and 'Auntie Aggie' just to tease her!) Apart from that we had great fun and did all the usual seaside things. Gordon, who was about my age, then about ten, was at Taunton School, and on Sundays he was supposed to wear his Eton jacket and long trousers and a mortar-board (was it? or was it a cap with a tassel? I forget.) Anyway he *hated* it, and each Sunday he had a row with his mother who insisted that he should dress in this for church. Poor lad!

We three girls had a holiday with Nana at Westcliff-on-Sea in 1915 just before Mother arrived in England with Eric. I remember that Nana read Dickens aloud to us, and that we made toffee and thoroughly enjoyed ourselves. We were very fond of Nana. About this time Great-Grandma Freeman died, she was Mother's Grandma. We had only seen the old lady once or twice, and hardly knew her or Great Aunt Fanny who lived with her. Later we saw a good deal of Auntie Fanny and grew very fond of her.

When Uncle Harry's and Auntie Elsie's three girls, Jean, Mary and Eleanor came to school they went to stay with Nana more often than we did, and so did Kitty Heberlet. They were more closely related to her than we were. She was our step-Grandma, she was Kitty Heberlet's step-sister's Aunt, and she was the other girls' great aunt on their Mother's side and their step-Grandma on their Father's! We were always joking about these family relationships and quoting them to our friends.

Some of the happiest times we spent were during the Easter holidays when we stayed on at school. Each year there were a number of girls who stayed at school for the Easter break as they had nowhere to go, and we all had enormous fun. The members of staff who stayed to look after us became our friends and not teachers, and put themselves out to give us a good time. Rules were relaxed, classrooms were turned into comfortable sitting-rooms with cushions and curtains. Sometimes rugs for the floor and armchairs and pictures could be found as well.

We went for day-long outings and picnics in the beautiful Kent countryside, and we produced concerts and plays in the evenings or had dances and sing-songs. There was no need to feel sorry for those of us who had to stay at the school for the holidays, we thoroughly enjoyed ourselves.

Nevertheless, some people were very sorry for us, and they issued 'general invitations' for children who had nowhere else to go. Phyllis and I were given such a one from Miss Horsfall in the summer of 1916 to go and stay with her at Stone Gappe, Cononley, near Keighley in Yorkshire. In her letter she promised us tennis, picnics, long walks, children, a farm, a large house and a large garden and the moors, and we were able to enjoy them all, though the holiday started badly for me. Long train journeys always upset me, and I was sick before I arrived in Leeds where we were met by Miss Horsfall. Here we went out of the station and, thinking we had arrived at our destination and finding my ticket hadn't been collected, I tore it up! Of course we were due to take a local train later on to Kildurick, and my ticket was still needed for that! Miss Horsfall was astonished by my stupid action but, all credit due to her, she didn't make too much fuss, and explained matters to the ticket collector, and showing Phyllis's ticket we were allowed through. After the next train journey we went by pony and trap to Cononley and Stone Gappe. I was very sick by this time and was put to bed, and there I stayed for two or three days. I was said to be suffering from a 'chill on the liver' or a bilious attack, which lasted for several days. I missed meeting visitors who came for raspberries and cream tea on the first day, and a picnic with Miss Horsfall's nephew and niece when Phyllis had the exciting adventure of paddling in a beck with them and 'tickling trout'. On Sunday morning Phyllis went to church with Miss Horsfall while I was still in bed; however in a day or two I recovered and was able to take part in all the activities that were arranged for us.

Stone Gappe was a very big house standing in large grounds. It had fifteen bedrooms, and Miss Horsfall talked of dividing it into two residences. Twice we were invited to lunch with Sir John and Lady Horsfall at 'Hayfield'. This was an even bigger house than their daughter's, and was set in large grounds with a boating lake. We found the luncheon party rather awe-inspiring, especially as there was a butler and a parlourmaid to wait at table. In the centre of the vast dining-table there was a 'turn-table' holding all the small items you might require – salt, sugar, butter, sauces – which could be turned so that one could reach them. There was what seemed to us a vast array of knives and forks and spoons at each place setting, and finger bowls at the end of the meal. After lunch we were allowed to go into the grounds with the grandchildren and mess about in the boat.

Miss Horsfall was very kind to us and her sister Mrs Walker had children of our own ages with whom we got on well, so in spite of being somewhat awe-struck and intimidated by all the grandeur of the house we enjoyed our holiday very much. Phyllis and I must have made a sufficiently good impression because all four of us were invited to spend part of the next Christmas holiday with the families. Dorothy and Eric stayed with the Walkers and Phyllis and I were again welcomed by Miss Horsfall. This time there was deep snow and most of our days were spent on two toboggans careering down a steep hill with a sunken fence and a deep snow drift at the bottom! We were bruised and wet but very happy!

During these holidays in Yorkshire we drove in a pony trap sometimes, but quite often we were taken in a motor car. This was my first experience of riding in a car. In 1916 none of our relations had acquired one.

In describing some of these holidays we had as children I have come to realize how lucky we were to have so many and such varied ones. In twelve years at boarding school I suppose I must have had nearly thirty-six holidays. Other people in our financial position would probably have had to be content with one week a year in Clacton or Southend-on-Sea. If I was not happy the cause was in me, not in my surroundings.

14

Guilt and Fear

I cannot remember exactly when it was, but I think it must have been sometime in 1913, when I was eleven years old, that I was summoned to Miss Hare's study to be given a talk on 'the facts of life'.

I was tall for my age, and it was believed that we would come to puberty early as we had been brought up in the tropics, so Miss Hare felt that I should be prepared in good time for the changes that would soon come. It was her habit to interview each girl individually when she felt it right for her to be told of the physical changes that would take place. We had no biology classes in school, but I suppose that in 'nature study' we had learned something about reproduction, but this was not related to human beings.

I well remember that interview with Miss Hare. She sat in an armchair, and I perched nervously on the edge of the sofa opposite her. I was shaking with fear as it was obviously a most solemn occasion, and as Miss Hare talked I was so overcome with emotion that tears slid down my cheeks and I wept silently. She was telling me how babies were carried and grew in their mothers' bodies until they were ready to come out into the world. I don't think that she gave me any explanation of how they got there in the first place, and what the father had to do with it. If she did mention it I must have suppressed the memory of it at once. What I do remember is that she gave me a description of how the 'nest' in the womb had to be prepared for the baby, and the walls had to be cleaned away and removed in blood. Then she talked about how I would feel tense and miserable and bad-tempered, but how important it was that I should not give way to these feelings, because the manner in which I behaved at that time would affect the development of my child.

I was so confused by it all that I came away with the belief that menstruation happened just once, in preparation for the baby, and that it lasted for nine months, and if you behaved properly all through that time you would have a perfect baby, and all would be well! I decided there and then that I would be a perfect 'model mum', always tidy, always punctual, with never a cross word or a miserable thought during my 'period'. Alas I was not prepared for the *monthly period* nor for all the stresses of puberty that I must go through before it would be possible for me to become a model mum.

Because I was far from being a model child, I was always being accused of day-dreaming, of being unpunctual, untidy, and careless in my school work. I was constantly in trouble and being given a 'stripe' for some minor offence. These stripes counted against you and when they were added up to some wicked total they meant that you would be given an 'imposition' when you had to write five hundred times, 'I must not . . .', or more seriously a 'report' to Miss Hare, or perhaps worst of all, banishment to the side table for meals.

The Dining Hall tables were each set for twelve girls, with a mistress seated at each end. You were allocated to a table and you sat there for all meals, except supper, and moved round a place each day so that you sat next to the mistress for two days, and had to make polite conversation with her. In addition there was the Top Table on the dais where Miss Hare sat facing the diners, with five girls sitting opposite her, and any guests who might be in the school on her left and right hand side. You took it in turns to go to the Top Table, according to your form and in alphabetical order. The youngest forms took the centre place, the middle school girls sat on either side, and the senior girls and prefects on the outer seats. Again one was expected to make polite conversation. When a girl had a birthday, or her parents were guests at the school, she went to the centre of the Top Table, and could invite four of her friends to join her.

In addition to these tables which had places set out with cutlery and silver, there were side tables, one on each side of the serving hatch, which were covered with a table cloth, but which were used for serving meals, and for the collection of dirty crockery. If you were in trouble and sentenced to banishment to the side table for meals, you had to collect your knife and fork and spoon and glass from your usual place, and take them, in front of all eyes, and in particular those of Miss Hare, and slink off in disgrace to sit by yourself at the side table. Your punishment might only be for one meal, or it might be for as much as a week. It was a humiliating experience .

My crimes were mostly for day-dreaming, lateness and untidiness, until one dreadful day when somebody – I think it must have been the school nurse – accused me of some unmentionable crime that she called 'self abuse'. This she assured me would lead to madness and eventual blindness. She told me that she knew I was practising this habit because of my listless day-dreaming and the fact that I had dark circles under my eyes. (If she had seen photographs of my mother taken when she was a young girl, and also when she was a young woman surrounded by her small children she would have seen that Mother too had sad eyes with dark shadows under them.) I was utterly bewildered by it all. I didn't know what I was supposed to have done. Had I done it in my sleep? If so, it was a terrifying thought that while you were asleep and unaware of your actions, you could do something so wicked that it would condemn you to madness and blindness. I knew that I had fantasised in bed sometimes and that occasionally I had felt a tingling between my legs, and had scratched and found the sensation pleasant. But this did not often occur, and was never a premeditated act.

There were three of us girls who the nurse accused of having committed this 'unspeakable crime'. One had been caught out doing something while she was sitting on the lavatory seat. But she hotly denied that she was doing anything improper, and was able to prove to the nurse's satisfaction that she was picking some hard skin off the sole of her foot. The other girl who was accused wrote at once to her grandmother who came down immediately on receiving the letter and took her granddaughter away for a few days, and when she returned no more was said about the 'sin' that she was supposed to have committed.

But I had no grandmother to turn to, and I was too bewildered even to mention my trouble to Dorothy or anyone else. So I was sent down to the cottage for 'treatment' to break me of this dreadful habit. I cannot remember who was in

99

charge at the cottage at this time. It was after the days of Miss Ray but I think that Miss Lovett was still there in the kitchen and the other one was probably Miss Reeve. Certainly it was no one to whom I could talk or ask questions. So there I was at the cottage, not ill, but in a state of bewilderment and unhappiness, waiting for I knew not what. Things were quite pleasant during the day, nothing was said and no explanations were given, but when it came to bedtime and I was undressed and ready for bed Miss Reeve came in with two flat pieces of wood and bandages and she bandaged each of my hands flat on to a board so that I couldn't do anything awful in the night. I lay there crying in shame and despair, a most miserable child.

How long the treatment lasted I don't remember – perhaps a week, when each night the boards and bandages were applied. At last the adults felt that I had learned my lesson and broken the vicious habit and that I was 'cured'. So I was allowed to go back to school. But the hurt went very deep, and the desperate feeling of guilt for a half-understood sin, and the fear of inevitable madness and blindness were always with me, at the back of my mind, for many years to come. I now knew that I could never have a child of my own. I could never be that 'perfect mother' that I had planned to be, and anyway I could not bear to think of a child of mine suffering as I was suffering. My fears were very real. I feared that I might walk in my sleep and murder somebody, or kill myself. The school stories that I read often had a 'ghost' in them which turned out to be one of the girls who walked in her sleep when the moon was full because she was under some severe emotional stress as she had committed some crime. I dreaded moonlit nights. The awful part was that I had no one to whom I could talk about the problem. It wasn't until Miss Lovett and Miss Reeve left and 'Nursie' Smart came to the cottage that I ever had any conversation about the subject. I remember that as I was having a bath while Nursie was present I plucked up my courage and asked her if I was ever allowed to touch myself 'there'.

'Well,' she said, 'it's better not to do so.'
'What about washing?' I asked.
'Oh, you can wash yourself with a flannel,' she told me.
'But I use the flannel for my face,' I objected.
'Then you must have a different one for there,' she said, and

I felt somewhat relieved. At last I had been able to hint at the dread subject, and it had been treated quite casually, without undue fuss and shame. We all loved 'Nursie' Smart. Her mother did the cooking and things were very pleasant at the cottage. They didn't stay long however, perhaps 'Nursie' was considered to be too soft with us.

15

Illness and the Yarrow Home

The year 1914 started badly for me. I had spent the Christmas holidays with Auntie Alice and Uncle Harry at their home, which at that time was in Mill Hill Lane, Derby, and then returned to school just before my twelfth birthday. Almost immediately I was sent down to the cottage because once more I was covered in spots. For several months I had had various forms of nettlerash or urticaria with pimples and blotches and many kinds of spots. It was now considered that these might be contagious and so I was isolated at the cottage with no one to talk to and nothing to do but read. I was very lonely and miserable. The cottage was still occupied by Miss Lovett and Miss Reeve, and all the entertainment that was offered me was an occasional walk with Miss Reeve.

My letter to Mother and Father on 28 January complains that I am 'all alone in one of the Cottage bedrooms, sitting by the fire (for I don't have to go to bed) reading, writing and thinking, but know (sic) one to talk to is not very nice.' On 5 February I reported that 'most of my spots have gone (the ones on my legs, arms and back) but a horrid rash has come on my chest.' On 12 February after stating that, 'I have onley got about twelve spots left' I also say 'I have given my heart to Jesus Christ and now I feel much happier and not so lonley.' (sic) On 18 February I wrote with pleasure that I was back at school, but on 15 March I was again taken down to the cottage, but this time in the bath-chair suffering an acute inflammation of the middle ear and running a very high temperature. I was very seriously ill, so serious was it that for about ten days I was nursed day and night by two uniformed nurses, and not just left to the care of Miss Reeve. I don't remember the name of the night nurse, but the day nurse, who was with me throughout the crisis and during my recovery, was Nurse Campbell, and I loved her dearly. She was kind and gentle and affectionate.

It was feared that I would have to have an operation to lance the abscess on the inner side of my ear-drum, and the nurses prepared me for that. They shaved the hair on the left hand side of my head, and Nurse Campbell gave me an enema. In spite of her reassurances and gentleness this seemed to be an assault and I wept in great distress throughout the proceedings, feeling that I was being punished once more for my unexplained wickedness. The mental anguish went very deep and the physical pain in my ear was of course very acute, and then – blessed relief! – the abscess burst of its own accord and there was no need for an operation to be performed. As the discharge cleared up and my temperature came down and I began to get better, visitors were allowed to come and see me.

Nurse Campbell with charming thoughtfulness bought me some pale blue hair ribbon, and she brushed my hair over the shaved surface and tied two plaits each with a blue bow at the end, and let them hang down on each side of my chest, so that I felt ready to face the visitors. Miss Hare came to see me and was very kind, and then Dorothy and Phyllis came, and I was very happy to see them. My hearing was badly affected at first and I was completely deaf in my left ear. It was feared that there might be permanent damage to the ear-drum but as the scar healed my hearing returned and remained almost as acute as in my good ear.

The night nurse was no longer needed, but I still had Nurse Campbell looking after me. At the beginning of April I was taken back to school (still in the bath-chair) as Miss Lovett and Miss Reeve were leaving the cottage at Easter. The school nurse was ill, so Nurse Campbell came with me, and I was put to bed in the nursery with a number of other girls who were sick, and Nurse Campbell was set to look after all of us. I was rather jealous as I felt that she was *my* nurse, and mine alone! However, she was soon to be replaced by Nurse Smart who arrived in preparation for her appointment as the new nurse at the cottage, with her mother who was to be housekeeper there. And now that I was up and about again and it was the end of term, it was arranged that I should be sent to the Yarrow Home, a convalescent home for children in Broadstairs. The plan was that I was to go there for a month. I was a bit apprehensive about it, and sorry that I was missing the Easter holidays with Dorothy and Phyllis at Nana's house in Woodford Green, but I had no choice in the matter. Nurse Campbell was to take me up to London to meet a party of children who were going from hospital to the Yarrow Home.

Nurse and I travelled up to Victoria and I managed not to be sick in the train! I hated the long Sevenoaks tunnel which was always filled with choking smoke in those steam-train days. I remember the journey well. We had made an early start in the morning and when we arrived at Victoria station Nurse thought that we should get a cup of tea and something to eat, so we went through some swing doors and entered what I now know must have been a bar in a public house. The room was full of men, standing about, or sitting on high stools at the bar, and as we came in all conversation stopped and they all turned and stared at a young and pretty nurse and a thin white-faced little girl. Nurse blushed scarlet, and we beat a hasty retreat. In 1914 women and children did not go into pubs. I think we went across the road to an ABC teashop and got our cup of tea and buttered currant bun. Then we went back to the station and met another nurse in charge of a party of boys and girls who were going to the Yarrow Home – and I said goodbye to *my* Nurse Campbell, and never saw her again.

I don't remember much of my journey to Broadstairs. I was shy and quiet and felt rather cold, and was coughing quite a bit, and was probably trying hard not to be sick. The boys and girls were about my own age, some younger, but none I think older than twelve or thirteen. They all seemed to be Londoners with Cockney accents. Some had crooked backs and limbs affected by rickets, others had scars on their necks where they had been operated for tubercular glands, while others were asthmatic. We were all a sickly lot, but I felt that they were more permanently affected by illness than I was.

When we arrived at the Yarrow Home I found it was a large red-brick building not unlike Walthamstow Hall, but it had two wings, one in which the boys were housed and one for the girls. I suppose there were about fifty children in each wing, if I remember rightly. On our arrival our party of new boys and girls were shown our dormitories, and told the rules. We slept in wards with about sixteen beds in each. There were day-rooms downstairs in each wing, and a common dining-room where we all had meals, where we sat boys on this side of the hall and girls on that. There were nice sized grounds where we were allowed to talk to each other, and as we were very close to the beach we spent most of every fine day there. We were certainly not allowed to bathe in the sea, but we paddled and we built sand castles and collected shells. I remember that I used to build flat areas of firmly beaten sand, perhaps four or five inches high and two or three feet across. Then I would cut the edges neatly to form the shape of a heart, a diamond or star, and then decorate the surface with pebbles, shells and seaweed, in the same way that we decorated flat mud cakes with flowers and leaves at school. None of the other children built castles quite like these, and I remember passers-by stopping and remarking on my creations. I wonder if I was influenced by Derbyshire well-dressings? Had I seen any at that time? Or heard about it from relations in Derbyshire? I don't know. I have certainly seen them since.

I remember one of the things that we did at the Yarrow Home; we became 'Scouts'. One of the boys was a Scout and his father presented us with staves, and we used to carry these about with us, and march with them on our shoulders, and use them to jump across streams and over obstacles . . . but my mind has run on to later days at the Yarrow Home.

On the first day that I arrived I unpacked my suitcase and found to my great surprise ten or twelve squares of linen with tapes sewn across two corners. I held these up to show the wardmaid who was helping me and said, '*Whatever* are these?'

She replied hastily, 'You'd better ask Sister,' and it gradually dawned on me that they were sanitary towels for use during that mysterious time when the 'period' came upon me (or as we used to say later, when 'The Curse has come upon me, cried the Lady of Shallot'), but at the age of twelve I hadn't yet reached puberty.

Unfortunately, as soon as I arrived at the Yarrow Home I fell ill again, this time with bronchial pneumonia, and I was put to bed in a little room by myself for – how long? – ten days or a fortnight. I was very lonely and unhappy. Gradually I recovered and went back to sleep in the ward with the other girls. I remember one night when I was first back in the ward I wanted to get up in the middle of the night and go to the bathroom, but I was too scared to go. There was a bright moon but in spite of the light coming through the windows in the corridor, because of my fear of the influence of the moon, I was too terrified to walk down the long passage to the bathroom. But I was also frightened of the consequences if I wet the bed, so finally I got out a leather-covered box intended for gloves or handkerchiefs that I had in my locker and used that as a chamber pot. I was able to empty it in the morning without being spotted, but it was in a soggy mess.

The children were quite friendly, but I was a bit of an odd one out; I was used to boarding-school food and rules, they were not. Many of them were very homesick, and they made a big fuss about the food. They used to make up songs and sing them. One I remember went to the tune of 'There is a happy land far far away':

> 'There is a Yarrow Home not far away
> Where nurses get the pip three times a day.
> Oh how the children yell
> When they hear the dinner bell,
> Oh how the eggs do smell,
> Three times a day!'

We were allowed to buy fourpennyworth of chocolate on Wednesdays and Saturdays, and the other children seemed to have plenty of pocket-money to spend. I had none. Then of course they had parents, many of whom came down on Sundays to visit them, while I had no one to come and see me, but waited anxiously for one letter a week from Mother and Father, and that was sometimes late.

By the end of the first month it was obvious that I was not well enough to return for the beginning of term. We had to queue up to see the doctor before we could be discharged, and we pinched our cheeks to try to make them rosy, and stuck out our chests to try to look fatter, but the verdict for me was 'Extension' for another month. We were weighed regularly, and given extra milk and cod liver oil, but I was given several extensions after that first one, so it was about four months later and nearly the end of the summer term before I went back to Sevenoaks.

Soon it was time for the summer holidays and we looked forward to spending them on Uncle Tom's farm in Sawley.

There was a feeling of anxiety and of foreboding among the adults and this was fully justified when on 4 August WAR WITH GERMANY WAS DECLARED. Everyones's life was changed.

I had a letter from one of the nurses at the Yarrow Home telling me that all the children had been sent back to their homes. I suppose that the building was put to another use in wartime.

16

The Great War – 1914–1918

As soon as war was declared changes took place at Sawley Grange. I remember two men coming one day to look at the horses. Rupert took them round the farm, and there and then they commandeered two of the best animals. They chose Kit, a strong chestnut horse who was used to take the milk-float round, and Dolly, a large, young, black cart-horse (who the farm hands called 'Sin' because of her tendency to bite.). The men, who were from the Army, left an older cart-horse to do the farm work, and Topsie, who Elsie and we children used to ride, (she was too old they said) and Rupert's hunter known as "Marcus Superbus, Prefect of Rome" (he was too valuable). I remember Rupert, who was a big, hefty young farmer, aged about twenty-one at the time, standing and watching as Kit and Dolly were being taken away, and there were tears in his eyes.

This of course was the beginning of many changes. The three boys, Joe, Frank and Rupert all enlisted: Joe and Rupert became commissioned officers, and Frank reached the rank of sergeant but didn't get a commission. Things were difficult for Frank as his wife was an officer in the Women's Army Corps and they were stationed at the same camp. Frank had to salute her if he met her walking with other men who were officers. Their marriage broke up and after the war Jean went to Australia taking their little daughter Bunty with her. Cousin Elsie's war service was working as a cook in a military hospital. Cousin Marjorie worked in a munitions factory. As the farm workers were called up and all his sons away, Uncle decided to retire from farming and move from Sawley Grange to Corner Croft in Sawley village. So for us children the war brought to an end our exciting farm holidays.

But we were not really very closely involved with the fighting forces. Father was in India and not called up, and Eric was only a child, too young for military service.

At school we had a Roll of Honour in each class-room, with the names of our relatives in the Forces. We three had the names of these cousins, and also of Uncle Arthur, Mother's youngest brother, who became captain, acting major, and won the Military Cross and Bar. We had photographs of all these relations in their uniforms and we begged from them their buttons and badges to show off to others.

We were proud of our connections in the Services, but we never got carried away to the extent of presenting white feathers to young men who had not enlisted, as many of our young contemporaries did. And we did not have to suffer the death of a near relative. Cousin Harold Pike was the only relation we knew who was killed in the war.

When I returned to school at the beginning of the autumn term in 1914 I was a day-boarder, living at the cottage so that Nurse Smart could keep an eye on me after my illness, and give me extra milk and porridge. This meant that I had to walk to school each morning down Holly Bush Lane where the troops were assembling for roll call. The men were in ranks on each side of the road, and I had to walk down the centre of the road while they were gathering and before they were called to attention. They used to greet me with wolf whistles and sly remarks like: 'Is it cold up there?' for I had grown so much during the time I was ill. Sometimes one would call out after me 'You are so far off the ground, be careful you don't fall!', or something about having to fetch a ladder to kiss me. I was very embarrassed and felt rather like Alice in Wonderland after she had grown so tall that she had to say goodbye to her feet.

The young soldiers were set to digging trenches in Knole Park in preparation for the real thing in France, and they drilled and had bayonet practice in the recreation ground next to the school. At Christmas time, that first year of the war, we made individual Christmas puddings in cookery class for – how many of the men? I cannot remember, but I know that we put a silver threepenny bit in each pudding, wrapped in a wad of greaseproof paper, and we hoped that each man found his 'lucky coin'. We children played in their half-dug trenches in the park, and crawled on our tummies through the connecting low passages. I shudder to think what might have happened to us if the earth had collapsed on us when we were underground. I was frightened at the time, but dared with the others to venture into the low, narrow tunnels. In the same way, earlier that year, I had crept into a tiny cave at Broadstairs, and had a moment of panic thinking that I was stuck and could never get out again.

As winter came on and the daylight faded earlier and earlier each day, the effect of the strict black-out was felt. There were no street lights, and everyone going out after dark wore luminous buttons or badges in the form of a cross, and white arm-bands. The buttons and crosses were painted with a substance that absorbed light during the day, and glowed with an eerie blue light in the darkness. On dark, moonless nights it was impossible to see pedestrians and you could easily collide with a silent person unless you heard footsteps or voices. We girls rarely went out beyond the school grounds after dark, and I had to hurry to get to the cottage before the daylight faded that first term. The black-out was strictly kept in the school. Previously we had enjoyed one electric light shining above the partition between two bedrooms and illuminating both cubicles. Now we had only one electric light in the centre of each corridor and this was a bulb that could be dimmed down to a feeble glow in the event of an air-raid.

When I returned to my cubicle, number 27 Lower East, I was as far away from the centre of light as it was possible to be, and I undressed in almost complete darkness. There were mice in my cubicle! I didn't mind – I encouraged them by feeding them with biscuit crumbs. But, just for fun, I rigged up a trap to see if I could catch one. This trap consisted of a box, tilted on its side, with a short string hanging down inside with a piece of food tied to the end of it. I lay in bed listening for the mouse. After some time there was a scrabbling sound and sure enough the string was pulled and the little mouse was caught! Of course he was not killed, not even hurt, but he spent the night jumping up and down in his prison, until the morning came when I opened the lid and watched with pleasure as he leaped out of the box and scampered away home!

Air-raid warnings were at first a cause for excitement and an excuse for not doing our homework. When the sirens wailed in the evening all the electric lights dimmed and we could not see to read or write. We had no air-raid shelters, and we gathered in the Dining Hall, centre of the building, and sang songs, or had a dance until the lights went up again. Sometimes we would creep out to look at the searchlights sweeping the skies for zeppelins. Later when our ack-ack defences were stronger there was the sound of heavy gunfire, and we could find pieces of shrapnel in the garden the next day. If a raid took place at night the girls from the upper corridors were instructed to come down into the room of the girl who slept below. Fortunately no bombs were dropped on Sevenoaks during the First World War, the zeps were making their way to more valuable targets in London. At one time there was a real fear of invasion, and preparations were made for evacuation if the enemy should land on the south coast. We were instructed to wrap up our clothes each night, in the counterpane, and to put in any treasures that we felt we must try and save, so that the bundle could be picked up if we had to flee in a hurry from fire or bomb or an invading force. I know that I used to pack my Bible in with my clothes and necessities; I felt that this would be a suitable thing to find in the 'pack' of a missionary's daughter!

We suffered from fears and anxieties of course, times of panic in the night, fear of invasion by the enemy, fear of starvation as the quality and quantity of food deteriorated. Many foods were rationed throughout the country. Meat, butter, sugar and cheese were in short supply for everyone, but in addition at our school, bread was also rationed. I suppose it was because the baker could not supply an unlimited amount to a large institution and deny his other customers. We were only allowed four rounds of a quartern loaf for each of us per day. We chose to have one round (two slices) for breakfast and also two slices for tea, and two rounds (four slices) for supper. Sometimes the slices were very thin, and we were often hungry, not starving, but still hungry. Supper sometimes consisted of four slices of dry bread and an apple, or a bowl of thin cabbage soup into which we crumbled our four slices of bread. We were weighed every month and if we lost too much weight we were given extra milk; if we gained weight we were taken off that extra milk.

The breakfast 'cereal' degenerated into a most peculiar semi-sweet cardboard-like substance called P.R. These initials stood for 'Physical Regenerator', I believe (or was it,

'Rejuvenator?'). We also had P.R. biscuits, which were equally unpalatable. One wartime speciality we *did* enjoy was 'honey-sugar', a very thick, runny substance which was very sweet and sticky. I believe that it had been skimmed off the top of the beer in the course of brewing, and so I suppose it was honey and yeast. We each had two little pats of butter each day, and a spoonful of honey-sugar or jam. This meant that we spread them both together on our bread. Before the war it had always been a choice of butter *or* jam, and we called it 'sky' if we had both together 'because it is so heavenly!' Jam, in wartime, was made of carrots and apple pulp and rhubarb or anything else that was available. Sugar was strictly rationed and we hankered for anything that was sweet. I, with two other girls, kept two hives of bees for Miss Hare, and in the winter after the honey had been extracted these were kept alive by feeding them with a pink candy, provided by the Government and off the sugar ration and labelled 'Unfit for Human Consumption.' We children sucked great chunks of this candy, undeterred by the notice, and I don't think we suffered any harm.

We did suffer anxiety about our relatives fighting in the Forces, and concern for any of the girls' parents travelling by sea. The boat on which Ivy and Patty Grundy's parents were sailing to India was torpedoed, but fortunately Mr and Mrs Grundy were rescued and came back to England. In 1915 Mother brought Eric home to school on the *Chussan* and they had to travel in convoy with other ships for protection. While they were at sea the Germans sank the passenger ship *Lusitania*, and Mother was very anxious throughout the voyages to England and back to India. In October she returned to India alone, without any of her children, on the *Kaiser-i-hind*, and we heard of her safe arrival with great relief.

I remember the anxiety and terror that I felt when the ship that Kitchener was on struck a mine off the Orkneys, and he went down and was drowned with all on board. When we heard the news of his death a terrible gloom fell on us all. Then the rumour spread that the whole thing was a false report, and I remember flinging myself down on my knees and thanking God with all my heart that Kitchener was safe! Only to be told the next day that it was not so – Kitchener was drowned. We believed at the time that he had been drowned in the English Channel. And then the rumour spread that Lloyd George and all the Cabinet had gone down with him! Why they should all have gone to sea together I do not know, but in our anxiety we were willing to believe the worst. It was a long time before ordinary people accepted the fact that Kitchener was dead. All sorts of stories were circulated asserting that he was alive and in France. One I remember told of a soldier who wrote in a letter from the Front, 'I know you collect stamps, so you will be interested in this one.' The one who received the letter took the stamp off very carefully and underneath was written 'K. of K. is here.' Kitchener of Khartoum had dominated our lives with the poster 'Your King and Country needs YOU!' with Kitchener's finger pointing straight at each and every one of us, and we could not believe that that dominant man was dead. I remember the poems that we were inspired to write during the war. They were stirring calls to arms and to deeds of bravery, with little understanding of the horrors that men were called upon to face in the trenches.

In the autumn of 1918 the whole country was suffering from an influenza epidemic and the school did not escape. Marjorie Milledge was one of the girls in our Form who helped me with the bees, and she died of pneumonia following 'flu, and a young member of staff, Miss Sharpe, in her first term as a school-mistress, also died. On Armistice Day, 11 November 1918, practically everyone in the school, children, teachers and domestic staff, was down with 'flu, or, having had it, had gone home to convalesce. On that day I remember there were only six of us still on our feet. It was pouring with rain. On hearing the news that the Armistice had been signed we went to a thanksgiving service held in the Parish church in the afternoon, and came back to school for tea. There we ate a whole quartern loaf of bread between the six of us, with all the butter and jam that we could find on the tables. Then we pulled up all the blinds, and drew back all the curtains, and put on all the lights in the school! THE WAR WAS OVER!

The next day we had to go back to rationing, and to the sensible use of electricity. And shortly afterwards I went down with 'flu myself.

17

Religion

As we were missionaries' children it was natural that religion should play an important part in our daily lives from early childhood. We were brought up to say our prayers regularly, and a grace was always said before meals. We were taken to church each Sunday, and hymn singing and family worship were part of our daily routine. Even in our games we conducted services, sang hymns and preached sermons. I remember one Sunday evening when I was about eight years old and I was all set to preach a sermon to the members of the family. Mounted on the seat of an armchair, and facing the congregation over the back of the chair I gave out my text from 'The Book of Ruth', but unfortunately pronounced the *oo* in 'book' as in 'boot', and the *u* in Ruth as in 'rush', and such laughter greeted my efforts that I got down from the pulpit in tears.

When we went to school we tended to keep up the habit of saying our prayers and reading the Bible, and the school fostered the latter by setting us to learn verses of Scripture by heart each day.

In 1909, when she was eleven years old, Dorothy formed a little society called BREM. Edna, Pattie, Ivy and I were all members with her. The letters stood for Bible Reading Every Morning, and we were supposed to write down every time we forgot to read our portion. Dorothy wrote in a letter to Mother and Father, telling them about BREM, 'Of course we have to think about what we are reading. Do you think it is right to do it, I mean do you think I ought to try and found this Society. I am just making up some rules.' Later we joined the Scripture Union and continued with our Bible reading. We also formed a society called OHMS, standing for On His Majesty's Service (this meaning God's service) and we took it all very seriously while it lasted.

I loved to sing hymns like 'Dare to be a Daniel, Dare to stand alone, Dare to have a purpose sure, And dare to make it known', with the promise that 'Many giants great and tall, stalking through the land, Headlong to the earth will fall, When met by Daniel's band'. It gave me a wonderful thrill, though it didn't seem to have much application to my daily life! I also loved:

> 'Pull for the shore, sailor.
> Pull for the shore!
> Heed not the rolling waves but bend to the oar!
> Safe in the Lifeboat, sailor,
> Cling to self no more,
> Leave the poor old stranded wreck
> And pull for the shore!'

Brave words, all, which gave me a momentary feeling of strength and victory, but didn't really help to solve my personal problems.

At times, in our letters to Mother and Father we gave them the information that we 'had given our heart to the Lord Jesus'. I know that Dorothy wrote it in a letter, and I also stated it when I was lonely or unhappy during one of my times at the cottage.

When I was staying with Auntie Alice and Uncle Harry Squirrell I used to be taken to the Band of Hope meetings, and when I was about eleven years old I signed the pledge 'to abstain from all intoxicating liquor as a beverage'. This card which I signed I later tore up, having been teased by the girls at school when I told them about it. So much for 'daring to be a Daniel'!

I also went to Sunday school with my cousin Marjorie during the holidays, and later I used to teach a Sunday school class of the youngest children if they were short of teachers.

At school girls in the Upper School, with Miss Hare's permission, held Bible study classes and prayer meetings which were open to any girl who wished to attend. I used to go to the prayer meetings, and with much trepidation and fear, would sometimes offer a prayer in a trembling voice.

115

In Sevenoaks we all went to church on Sunday mornings. When we were in the Lower School we did not go out again in the evenings but we had hymn singing in the schoolroom. We sang with great gusto all the well-known missionary hymns such as *From Greenland's icy mountains*, and, when we were very young, we loved to choose special hymns that we could relate to. We sang 'Coming, coming yes we are, Coming, coming from afar' and also 'We are travellers on a journey, A journey to a better land', in which people from different lands joined the procession singing, 'I from China . . .' and 'I from Africa', each group singing lustily of the country from which its members came. How I envied the girls who had to sing solo such words as 'I from islands of the Main'. I didn't fully understand it, but I knew that Marjorie Milledge (from Madagascar) and Merne Graham (from the Philippines) had to lift their trembling voices by themselves, while I was in a large group of singers from India.

When we went to church the largest number of us attended the Vine Baptist Church, while a few girls went to the Parish Church. Some may have attended a Methodist Church, but I believe that for some reason Miss Hare disapproved of the minister of the Congregational Church and the girls from there had to come to the Baptist Church. All those who had been baptized or had joined the Church stayed for communion after the morning service.

During the first part of my school-days the minister at the Baptist Church was Mr Feltham, but in later years Mr Gray became our minister. He was very popular, as he was young, energetic and more outgoing.

It was on 7 November 1915, just before Mother returned to India after she had put Eric in Eltham College, that I whispered to her in the Reception Room at Walthamstow Hall that I wanted to be baptized and join the Church. I suppose that the preacher on that Sunday had made an appeal to all to give themselves to Christ. I don't remember now his text or his message. I remember sitting on the settee on Mother's left side, with Phyllis on her right, and she had an arm round each of us. She was tightly corseted and physically stiff and unyielding, but she was doing her best to express her love for us, and to understand my wishes. As soon as I said that I wanted to be baptized Phyllis whispered that she 'wanted to do the same as

116

Joyce', but she was only eleven years old and Mother said hastily that she was too young to decide, and that she must wait for a year or two. To me she said that she was very glad, and that she would tell Miss Hare and Mr Feltham and the Reverend Charles Wilson at the Mission House, and that it would be arranged.

And so the wheels were set in motion, and moved inevitably on to the day of my baptism. Whatever emotion had encouraged me to tell Mother that I wanted to be baptized had evaporated, and now I had no sense of elation or joy, but I was consumed by anxiety and fear. Mother had left the country, I could no longer talk to her, and there was nobody to whom I could turn. Merne Graham, a girl from my Form who was about four years older than I, had expressed a desire for baptism at about the same time, and we were interviewed together by Miss Hare, and arrangements were made for us to be baptized at the same service.

I had no doubts concerning the genuineness of Merne's conversation. Her father was a Scottish Presbyterian missionary working in the Philippines, and Merne was a quiet, deeply religious girl, who found her school work difficult, but seemed to know where she stood spiritually. I sometimes was able to help her with her homework (I remember explaining osmosis to her as she had failed to understand the lesson) but I didn't dare ask her to help me solve my spiritual problems. We went together to see Mr Feltham, the minister, but I think that he felt that 'from a babe thou hast known the sacred Scriptures that shall make thee wise unto salvation', (as Father had written in the Bible that he had given me) and was probably quite unaware of the turmoil in my heart and mind.

Merne and I were invited to the Mission House in London to see Mr Wilson who was the Foreign Secretary of the Baptist Missionary Society. We had tea with him and I was asked to pour out, and I was so nervous that my hands shook and I spilled tea in all the saucers. Mr Wilson talked kindly to us, and told us what would take place at the baptism service which he was going to come to Sevenoaks to conduct, and then we had prayer with him before we left and returned to school. I was still very unhappy but there was nothing that I could do and no one whom I dared tell how unfit I was for baptism. Everyone else seemed to be so confident that all was well.

On Monday 27 March 1916, when I was fourteen and Merne was eighteen, we were baptized at the Vine Baptist Church, Sevenoaks. We wore the most unbecoming heavy white piqué dresses down to our ankles, weighed down with little lead weights at the bottom, with an elbow-length cape of the same white piqué as the gown, round the shoulders, and also weighted round the bottom. All this was to ensure that when the garments were under the water they would not ride up, and that when we emerged from the baptistery the clothes would not cling too tightly and reveal the figure. Our hair was plaited in tight plaits, with no ribbons or bows. Miss Hare sat between us during the service, and I remember that I was picking nervously at a darn or rough spot on my baptismal gown, and Miss Hare put her hand over mine to stop me. I remember the experience vividly, but instead of looking back on the occasion as an old woman I will give the actual 'child's eye view' written at the time in letters to Father and Mother. These of course did not express my deep anxiety and guilt, but just describe the events:

On 10 March 1916 I wrote:

'A week last Saturday I went to the Cottage. The day before Merne and I went to see Mr Feltham. He was very nice to us. A few days later Merne got her letter of permission from her father. Last week I was in bed so I could not write. But I am alright now! Last Sunday Miss Hare told us that our baptism would be on Monday 27 March. I am afraid that it will be over by the time you get my letter. But it can't be helped! Edna is going to help us get ready, I have invited Mona Williams, and Dorothy Passmore, Jean Gillison, Bella Pullar and Marjorie Milladge, four girls in my Form, and in our meeting, to come. Of course most of the girls who have joined the church will come; and also Irene Passmore, an old girl who is coming down.' (The rest of the letter concerned other matters including, 'Last Saturday Dorothy and Phyllis went out to tea to the Taylor-Smiths. I could not go because of my cold.')

22 March 1916:
'Please excuse pencil but I am in bed not feeling very well. O, really I am alright just a bit funny! But I will be alright and up to-morrow . . .
Next Monday we begin exams, as well as our baptism. I have written to Uncle (T. Smith) to tell him about it . . .
The weather has turned very cold again . . .
Phyllis and I have been wanting to get some more white mice! It would be ripping if we could! We *may* be allowed to, but I have not asked Miss Hare yet . . .'

29 March 1916:
'My dear Mother and Daddy,
Thankyou very much for the letters that we got yesterday. I have been baptized, last Monday. Mr Wilson did come down. Nearly all the Upper School were present. We had our exams; in the afternoon so as to be free at the time. Edna helped me, and Pattie, Merne. There was also a woman in the Church there. We got dressed in the vestry. Before we went to the church we had a few words with Mr Wilson in Miss Hare's sitting room. He told us what to do etc., Mrs Feltham came in and talked to us after we were dressed. Our dresses were white. A white skirt and a sort of little cotton coatee over it. They were not very bad. Just before we went in Mr Wilson came in and we prayed. Then we went in. We sat in the front row, with Miss Hare between us. I was baptised first. But Mr Wilson first gave us a very nice talk. He was not at all formal but just said, "My dear Joyce, I baptise you . . . etc." The water was very cold, or rather it felt so to me! But we soon got warm in the vestry, which was heated to an awful heat! I forgot to tell you that Mr Taylor Smith was there, a soldier, and one or two others beside the whole Upper School. Ethyline Scott had to play the harmonium as there was no one else. Just as we were being baptised the people burst into singing, "Oh, happy day." It sounded very strange as the water rushed into my

ears, and I felt very dazed. It was a freezing cold night, and it was snowing quite hard, so Miss Hare had ordered a cab for us. Directly we got home we had some hot 'bovell' and were packed in to bed. But all the same I had a bad cold yesterday, though it is much better to-day.'

Much of the rest of the letter is taken up with news of the snow, and anxiety about the exams which 'we started last Monday and are now in the thick of them' and then the news that, 'The cook has left, so the girls have to do the cooking with the help of Miss Heenan. Every one is awfully bussy now a days. Last Thursday I helped cooking the dinner for the school. It was rather fun!!' (The quotations are given as written, spelling mistakes and all.)

There was no expression of joy because of my baptism, and in truth I had no such feelings to express. I was overwhelmed with anxiety and fear that my actions had been hypocritical. Later when I was given 'the right hand of Fellowship' and welcomed into 'the Membership of the Church' it was no better, and when I stayed to take part in the communion service I was racked with fear that I might be taking it 'thoughtlessly' and so be 'guilty of the Body and Blood'. There was no peace for the wicked, and no happiness in fellowship, and so, after several years, I let my membership of the Church lapse (much to my Father's distress) and did not have it transferred as I moved from place to place. As the years went by I rarely had the courage to take part in the communion service again, and it took me a long time to find any comfort in the rite.

18

Examinations

We had written examinations at the end of each term and the results were given in our reports which were sent to our parents. I never did very well in these exams, partly because I was so often away from school because of illness. When I returned I felt quite lost in the lessons and couldn't follow them. This disheartened me, and I drifted along in a dream and didn't try to catch up, and anyway I always lost marks because of my bad spelling. I never knew where my actual 'place' was in the Form because Miss Hare did not believe in encouraging competition, but I felt sure that I was always somewhere at the bottom of the class.

When Miss Hare became Headmistress an arrangement was made that the school should be inspected by the University of London and then allowed to take the Junior and Matriculation Standard examinations set by that university. In 1917 Dorothy sat for Matric., and I took Junior London. Phyllis at the same time took the Higher music exam. I was in a terrible state of anxiety about the exam, and realised that I knew very little about the subjects that I was to be tested in. In a letter to Mother and Father I wrote on 17 May, 'Only four more weeks before French oral. Oh help! and about 3 more weeks after that Junior proper. I am so afraid that I shall fail! Oh dear I wish O Mother, Daddy I am in such a stew about it. O I wish you were here to chear me up.'

On 6 June 1917 I wrote,

> 'Last Saturday we had French Oral. Do you know Miss Little thinks that I have passed as Mr Ripman did not say that I was bad and he would have done so if I had failed.

We had lessons until lunchtime and then the Matrics had their Oral. They took the whole of the rest of the morning and we had to have ours carried on till after dinner. It would be difficult to express my feelings that day. In the morning I woak up with a feeling of excitement, which became the feeling of going away for the holidays. Then at lunch I felt angry and weepy by turns! If anyone spoak to me I either snapped them up or had much ado to keep from crying. Then at dinner I was absolutely hilarious and rushed about like a mad thing; but when it came to the thing I was an absolute wreack!.'

The letter goes on to describe the oral examinations in which I had to talk about the 'Anne of Cleaves House in Sussex:' 'Now I can think of piles of things that I could have said but at the time I *couldn't*!' Mr Ripman remarked to Miss Little afterwards that 'Miss Wilkins was very nervous, and so I have marked her a little leniently' – but of course I failed – hopelessly. I wrote, 'Oh Mother! Oh, Daddy, I have failed in Arithmatic, History and French.' In consequence I did not get a Junior London Certificate. I may have scraped through in Geography and Literature. I cannot remember now. All I know is that the final result was a failure. In giving the results I wrote as a postscript to the letter 'O still love me although I have disappointed you, please.'

Dorothy passed splendidly with Honours, with Distinctions in Botany, History and Special Credit in oral French. She left school in 1917 and went up to Bedford College in the University of London and obtained a B.Sc. degree in Psychology in 1920.

Phyllis passed her music exam and, if I remember rightly, got 100 per cent in her paper on the rudiments of music and high marks in the practical. But as for me, the worst thing that happened was that Miss Hare decided that I must stay down in the same Form and take Junior London again next year. That meant that I was now to be in the same form as Phyllis, and I was two and a half years older than she. Fortunately we were good friends, but it was a very difficult time for both of us. Poor Phyllis could not fully enjoy her success while I was bemoaning my failure.

On 19 September 1917 I wrote to Mother and Daddy,

'Oh, is there? IS there any chance of you coming home before Christmas? O! if only you could! I heard a rhumer that you might! O! *Do! DO! DOOOO!!!* School is so horrid this term with no Dorothy, and being in another Form and doing such easy work – you see it is the work I did a year ago – and of course in the subjects I passed in it is too easy. Still I'll have to lump – but oh, is it so, *so beastly!* I think I should sooner of left than come back to *this*. None of my old Form take any notice of me – and I feel *awfull*. And oh but I am only down in the dumps at present – take no notice of it – I will be happier and more settled down next week and then I shall write chearfully!'

And so it was. On 22 September I wrote,

'I find I am not the eldest in the Form – about 4th or 5th eldest so it is not so bad as it might be is it? After all it is not half so bad as I expected in fact it is quite nice being in Phyllis's Form.'

In that letter I also say, 'Do you think it is possible for you to come over before Christmas? oh *do!* I simply dream about it all day long!' Why I expected Mother and Father to be able to come back for Christmas 1917 I do not know. Certainly Father's furlough was due, but travelling was so dangerous that no one would undertake it unnecessarily. The ship that Ivy and Pattie Grundy's parents were sailing on was torpedoed, and though they were rescued they spent hours in an open boat and Mr Grundy's hand was badly crushed. So my hopes of seeing Mother and Father soon had to be repressed. They did not come back until after the war was over, in 1919.

Phyllis and I soon settled down together in the same Form. She had her own friends of course, but I was often invited to share in their activities, and Phyllis and I did many things together. We were partners in tennis and were quite good at the game and played in the School Six. She had her music, both piano and violin, and often played at school concerts, but I was often asked to recite, and later learned solo singing and sang in the choir and in performances of operettas. I sang soprano of course, I had not the ear to keep an alto part. We both took special drawing and painting lessons with Miss Staveley. There is a letter from me dated 29 September 1917 when I am asking Mother and Daddy about drawing lessons.

> 'What about drawing? Are we both to learn? It would be an awful lot £4.4 a term! If either of us has to leave off I think it had better be me – for Phyllis has really a very good talent for Drawing – and she easily beats me hollow! In fact she beats me in *everything*. She is a *genious* that girl! There is nothing that she is not good in, lessons, games, music, Drawing, and singing. O, she *is* lucky!! I wish I had half her brains! Well it is no good bemoaning something that I have not got is it?'

So now Phyllis and I worked together as we prepared to take the Junior London examination in 1918. I was following the same syllabus for a second year, and in many cases studying the same set books, and the same period in History, and so, at the age of sixteen, I gained an Honours Junior London Certificate with distinction in English Literature, History and Botany. Phyllis of course passed too, with distinction in History, English Literature, and oral French, but she was only just fourteen. Now at last I had a Certificate, but it really was no use to me except as a preparation for sitting the Matriculation examination in two years time.

I remember very little about school work during those two years, and for some unknown reason there are no letters from us to Mother and Father during 1918. Some of our letters may have been lost due to enemy action during the war, but I do not know why none of them survived.

I was busy bee-keeping during those years. Miss Hare bought a hive of bees and Miss Burt instructed Marjorie Milledge, Jean Gillison and me how to look after them. We had a bumper harvest of honey in 1918, and took several swarms. Sadly, Marjorie died in the influenza epidemic in November 1918, but Jean and I continued to look after Miss Hare's bees, and in 1919 she gave me a hive of bees for myself. I remember being present at the inaugural meeting of the Kent Bee-

Keepers Association which took place in the school grounds in 1919.

Father and Mother returned to England in 1919. I cannot remember when they came, I think it must have been sometime in the autumn, I was working for the Matric exam. I know that I was very depressed and frequently in tears. They took a furnished house called 'Suningdale' near the station in Sevenoaks for a short time, and then they moved to 3, Eardly Road, and shared a house with Mr and Mrs Blackburn and their three daughters, Chyrstobel, Gwendolin and Emmeline who all attended Walthamstow Hall. The girls were much younger than we were. Emmeline was just entering kindergarten when I was in my last year at school. In fact at the time I was acting as a pupil-teacher in the kindergarten after my exams had finished and before I knew the results. My boast has always been that I taught Emmeline her first steps in learning to read in the kindergarten, because in later years she became a highly successful and very popular Headmistress of the school!

Phyllis and I took the exam in 1920, and during the months of preparation I was planning my future. There was a suggestion that I should try to get into the House of Education in Ambleside, and train as a kindergarten teacher – but it depended on the results of my examination. And, of course, the inevitable happened – Phyllis passed Matric and I failed to get it.

Poor Phyllis! It was a particularly difficult situation for her because her success was again blighted by my failure. Her future plans were to take Oxford Entrance and read for an Honours Degree in English. My plan now was to go out to India with Father and Mother, and Oh! how Phyllis *longed* to be allowed to go out to India too! But it seemed that I was to be rewarded for my failure, and she was to be left behind in England still pining for home life, for her talent was too great to be wasted, she must go on to further education.

So I left school in 1920 and Phyllis stayed on in the sixth form as Head Girl during Miss Hare's last year as Headmistress. The sixth form at Walthamstow Hall was not large enough to give her all the tuition she needed in preparation for Oxford, so at the end of that session, taking with her all the major prizes that the school had to give, Phyllis left Walthamstow Hall in 1921 and joined the sixth form of Clapham High School for

Girls (one of the schools in the Girls' Public Day School Trust) and took her Oxford Entrance Examination from there. In 1922 she went up to Somerville College, and read for an English honours degree.

19

Plans for the Future

During my last year at school I was very depressed and was frequently in tears. Father and Mother were 'home', but I seemed unable to make contact with them when they were actually here. In a way it had been easier to write my feelings than to speak them. Mother was either shy and withdrawn or she was irritable and cross with us for petty faults. Father was a stranger; though cheerful and friendly he found my depression very distressing and difficult to deal with. When the results of the examination were known and it was seen that I had failed to matriculate, Father and Mother decided that the only thing for me to do was to give up any idea of training or further education and to return to India with them (with the unspoken thought that it was not worth spending money on any training for me as I would probably do the natural thing and get married and not try to be a career woman). But though I had failed to get the necessary qualifications I wanted to do *something*, but what could I do? I had been acting as pupil-teacher in the kindergarten, but all hope of training at the House of Education in Ambleside had faded with my poor exam results. I was offered a job as a sort of 'nanny' with an English family in Switzerland, but was much too depressed and nervous to dream of going abroad by myself.

I read a book called *Careers for Women* in which there was a chapter written by Elsie Fogerty, the Principal of the Central School of Speech Training and Dramatic Art, on the career of teacher of elocution, or of Speech and Drama (or as Miss Fogerty might have called it, Voice and Diction). I had, during my school days, done a good deal of reciting of poetry and some solo singing, and it seemed that there might be a possible career in this for me. Then in the final paragraph of her article Miss

127

Fogerty wrote something about stammering being treated and defective speech corrected. On reading this I decided immediately that this was what I wanted to do – to treat speech defects and cure stammering! I had had a friend in my Form, Doris Hancock, who stammered. She was a day-girl and I had been invited to stay with her over an Easter weekend. Her parents had been very grateful that I appeared to be very patient with her and 'good for her', and that I was able to help her.

Then I remembered with interest the deaf-mute children from Mary and Ethel Hare's school, and began to realize that their faulty speech was due to their deafness and not, as in the case of a child with a cleft palate, due to something being wrong with their organs of speech. I remembered my own lisping and tongue-tie, and so began to take a real interest in thinking of becoming a 'remedial speech trainer'. Father agreed that I could have one year's training if that could be arranged, and I left school in the hope of doing something in that line. However, Father was worried about me going to the Central School for it was a stage school and he was afraid that I might want to go on the stage! (If I had done, think what a career I might have had! At about that time Lawrence Olivier and Peggy Ashcroft, were students at the Central School, and there were many other successful actors on stage and screen who trained there.) However, I assured him that the teachers' training course was quite separate from the stage course and he agreed that I might go and see Miss Fogerty.

So in July 1920 I said goodbye to my school friends and we presented each other with photographs of ourselves taken especially for the occasion, and we hoped that we would remember each other for the rest of our lives! (Sometimes I came across one of these photographs and wonder 'who on earth was that?') And as a family we said goodbye to Sevenoaks too, as Father had rented a furnished house at 9, Drakefield Road, Balham. This we shared with the Jarrys. We had separate establishments, but we had to share the use of the kitchen and bathroom. Father and Mr Jarry were often away preaching, on deputation for the Baptist Missionary Society. Mother and Mrs Jarry were friends of many years standing, but they still did not call each other by their Christian names, and Mother

Joyce aged 18, on leaving school

129

was worried by 'what will Mrs Jarry think?' if we wanted to do anything a bit out of the ordinary.

I went for an interview with Miss Fogerty at the Central School of Speech Training and Dramatic Art, which had its class-rooms in the outer curves of the Royal Albert Hall, Kensington Gore. (I seem to remember that the number 54 bus took me from door to door, with no anxieties about trains and the underground.)

In 1920 the training courses offered by the school were of two kinds, a course for students who hoped to go on the stage or into films, and another for pupils who wished to become teachers of speech and drama. The duration of each of these courses was two years. (Shortly after this they were extended to three years.)

I told Miss Fogerty that I only wanted to take a one-year course before I went to India, and that I wanted to be trained as a remedial teacher. She said that she had no such course, and that in her article in *Careers For Women* she was merely indicating that *she* could treat stammerers and people with defective articulation. She had a clinic at St Thomas' Hospital in London where she treated such cases. However, she considered my situation and after some thought agreed that she would arrange a special course for me. I was to attend all the anatomy and physiology lectures that were given to the teachers in their first and second years, all the voice classes with Dr Aiken, and the diction classes with her, and both first and second year phonetics with Mr Ripman, (my French oral examiner, now called 'Uncle Walter' by the Central School students), a movement class, and a craft class. I could not take mime, dancing or drama as I was also to attend Miss Fogerty's speech clinic at St Thomas' Hospital, and Dr Scripture's clinic at the National Hospital for Nervous Diseases. So it was agreed between Father and Miss Fogerty that I could have a year at the Central School and sit an examination for a certificate that would qualify me to act as a 'remedial speech trainer' or a 'stammering instructor'!

Father and Mr Jarry returned to India in the autumn of 1920 to be without us for a year. Mrs Jarry stayed in England to settle Edna in her nursing career, and Gordon into university and Freda, who was much younger than we were, into school. Mother stayed behind so that I could have my year at the

Central School before sailing back with her on the *SS Circassia* in October 1921.

I took my examinations at the end of the academic year and obtained the necessary special certificate, and an International Phonetics Certificate. I also got the first prize in the first year verse-speaking competition, which took place in the empty Albert Hall, with the examiners sitting in seats high up on the other side of the building. I came second in the 'Uncle Walter's' story-telling competition for which he gave an opal as the first prize. This prize went to Irene Sadler who became a professional verse speaker, travelling round the country with John Masefield and other poets when they were on lecture tours and illustrating their lectures with poetry reading.

Dorothy passed her B.Sc. exam and we were in the Albert Hall again, but this time when it was packed with people, to see her 'capped and gowned' (and the Prince of Wales receive an Honorary Doctorate). Dorothy wore my primrose yellow frock, and grey silk stockings and suede shoes for the occasion. The Prince of Wales wore a scarlet gown and a flat black velvet hat.

During the summer I went to Manchester to help Auntie-Miss-Moody who was a nanny and general mother's help to a very wealthy Jewish family. They had seven children, the eldest boys were grown-up, but we were responsible for the care of the three youngest who were still of nursery age. Auntie-Miss-Moody was also a 'confessor' and friend to the adolescent boys, and even the young men came to her for advice. We all had a summer holiday together in Llandudno.

In October 1921 we sailed to Bombay on the *SS Circassia*. Mother and I were to return to Cuttack where the B.M.S. had a boarding school for Eurasian boys and girls. They offered me a teaching post in the kindergarten for a year while their missionary teacher was home on furlough.

So the wheel had turned full-circle, and once more I was back in India with my parents, now with my childhood behind me.

EPILOGUE

Father, Mother and I came back to England in 1926. We left Calcutta in the midst of riots, and landed in England in the middle of the General Strike.

Father retired from the Baptist Missionary Society, and he bought a house at 21, Whitmore Road, Beckenham, Kent, which was then still quite a rural area.

Father still did some preaching on behalf of the B.M.S. but he felt restless and useless, and soon took on the pastorate of Camberwell New Road Baptist Church, which was without a minister. He conducted Sunday services and week-night meetings, travelling between Camberwell and Beckenham for a number of years. He died in 1957 in his eighty-ninth year. Mother died in 1958 at the age of eighty-six.

Dorothy took her B.Sc. at Bedford College, London, and followed that by taking a Social Science Diploma, and then started medical training, which it had always been her ambition to do. She started by attending evening classes at Birkbeck College while she herself lectured during the day on anatomy and optics to art students at the Royal Drawing Society. When she had passed her theoretical exams and the time had come for full-time study, she did her clinical training at the Royal Free Hospital London School of Medicine for Women. Throughout her student days she acted as guardian for Eric, and had a very hard struggle financially. The money that she had to borrow from charitable funds was all paid back by her when she started earning. She qualified as a doctor with MB.BS of the University of London. She then had a training analysis and became a psychiatrist. She was appointed by the London County Council to the medical staff of Horton Mental Hospital. After her marriage she went into private practice.

She married Professor Reginald Otto Kapp, and they had a

son and a daughter. Dorothy died in 1966 at the age of sixty-eight, and Reggie died three days later.

Phyllis obtained an Oxford M.A. and taught in a number of schools including the Merchant Taylors School for Girls at Great Crosby, and the North London Collegiate School. She was awarded a Francis Mary Buss Scholarship to study education in Sweden for six months. On her return she was appointed Headmistress of the King Edward Sixth Grammar School for Girls, Louth. Finally she was appointed to be one of Her Majesty's Inspectors of Schools, and held that office until she died in 1962 at the early age of fifty-eight.

My brother Eric Gordon took his MB.BS and qualified as a doctor of medicine. He married Honor Elizabeth Cooper Harvey who was also a newly-qualified doctor and they went out as missionaries to the people of the Khond Hills in Orissa, India. Here they built and worked in the Moorshead Memorial Hospital. During their furlough in this country they both studied for and obtained the higher degree of M.D. of the University of London. Eric specialized in Tropical Medicine, and Honor in Obstetrics and Gynaecology.

They had three sons. In 1951 when the boys were of school age, they returned to England. Eric worked in Dorking and later in York as a Consultant in Geriatrics. He was elected to the Fellowship of the Royal College of Physicians of London. Honor died in 1986 just before her eightieth birthday. Eric died in 1988 in his eighty-first year.

I stayed at home in Beckenham for a number of years after we returned from India. I did the cooking and the house-keeping for the family, and was occupied with the Girl Guide Movement. I ran a Guide, a Ranger and also a Cadet Company, and for a time was the Kent County Captain. In the mid 1930s I had a course of psychoanalysis and felt more able to take on a proper job.

I went as an observer to speech clinics in schools, and took a course of lectures in phonetics at University College, London. I was then offered employment as a speech therapist in the Education Service of the London County Council, and was given two clinics, one in Camberwell and one in Norwood, for the treatment of children who stammered or had defective articulation due to cleft palate or other causes. I also had an evening class for adults who stammered at the Hugh Middleton Institute in Holborn.

Dr. M.M. Lewis, a lecturer in the Department of Education in University College, Nottingham established a Department of Spoken Language at the College in 1938 and I was advised to apply for a post and was appointed as a part-time assistant lecturer and speech therapist in his department. So I went to Nottingham in 1938, and later when the College became the University of Nottingham, I was awarded an Official Degree of the University in 1955 for a thesis on 'Rhotacism.'

During the years that I was in Nottingham I lectured to students in the Department of Education who were in training to become teachers, and also to students in Paton College who were training for the ministry. I gave lectures on the phonetics of English to students from overseas.

As a speech therapist I was available to offer individual help to any member of the staff or any student who suffered from stammering or any speech defect or had problems of voice production.

I was allowed time to work in the local hospital and there I treated patients with voice and speech disorders or the loss of speech following a stroke. I remained on the staff of the University for twenty-five years until my retirement in 1963.

I was a member of the committee that established the College of Speech Therapists in 1944 and was made a Founder Fellow of the College. I served on the Council of the College for a number of terms as Vice-Chairman, and Chairman, and later as President, I was on the Examinations Board and an examiner until my retirement.

Now I am an old woman and the only member of our immediate family still alive to write this record. I often wonder why?

POSTSCRIPT

A Child's Eye View is, of course, narrow, limited, biased and entirely self-centred. So to what extent can it be considered to be a 'true' picture of my childhood days so many years ago? How would my contemporaries have viewed the world in which we all lived? I was an unhappy child and that coloured my view of things. On the whole, were the other girls at our school happier in the situation in which we found ourselves? Some certainly were, but I think that many of us felt the deep sense of deprivation because of our separation from our parents. The children had to be sacrificed because the parents had answered the 'call'. (How deeply disturbing I found the story of Abraham, willingly preparing to sacrifice his son Isaac to the Lord.) Now, as an adult I can feel more sympathy for the parents – and Abraham. I realise too that many of our teachers, including Miss Hare, were well aware of our problems and tried their best to give us a 'home' as well as school.

It must be remembered that this book cannot really be what it set out to be – a child's eye view – because it is written by an adult looking back through a long tunnel of recollection some sixty, seventy, eighty and more years after the events recorded. How then can it really tell the truth? All I know is that the details are recorded as I remember them, and that they reveal something of my feelings at the time of which I write.

I am anxious, however, to express my real appreciation of the school that I attended for twelve years, and my gratitude for all the advantages that it gave me in preparing me for life. In 1938 I was proud to attend the centenary celebrations of the school and to acknowledge my debt to the institution and to many of the devoted staff who tried to help me during my difficult childhood years. In 1988, one hundred and fifty years after the establishment of Walthamstow Hall as 'A Home and School for the Daughters of Missionaries', I was thrilled to go

135

back to Sevenoaks and to see the flourishing, modern High School for Girls, and to know that I am one of many hundreds of women who are grateful for the privilege of having been at Walthamstow Hall.

1838–1988

The present badge of Walthamstow Hall depicting: Sevenoaks, the Torch of Knowledge, a Manchet (a symbol used in heraldry to signify a female institution) and the Ship that Sails the Seven Seas.
Non Palma Sine Pulvere
(No palm (ie. award, prize) without dust.)

After eight years in India, Father came back to England in 1919. This photograph was taken to celebrate our parents' Silver Wedding in 1920

137

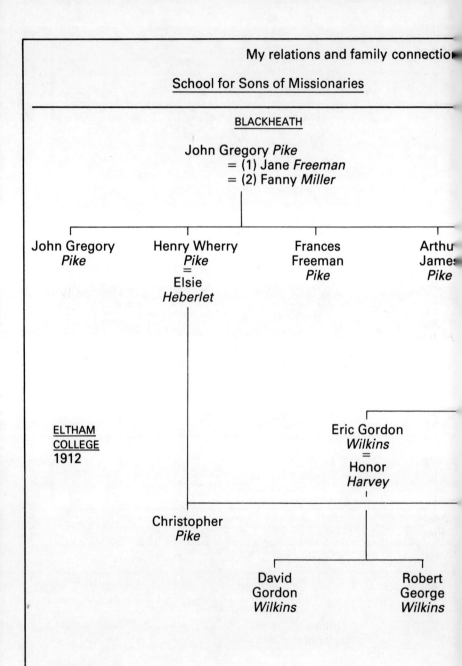

My relations and family connection

School for Sons of Missionaries

BLACKHEATH

John Gregory *Pike*
= (1) Jane *Freeman*
= (2) Fanny *Miller*

John Gregory *Pike*

Henry Wherry *Pike* = Elsie *Heberlet*

Frances Freeman *Pike*

Arthur James *Pike*

ELTHAM COLLEGE 1912

Eric Gordon *Wilkins* = Honor *Harvey*

Christopher *Pike*

David Gordon *Wilkins*

Robert George *Wilkins*

Nine boys

138

School for Daughters of Missionaries

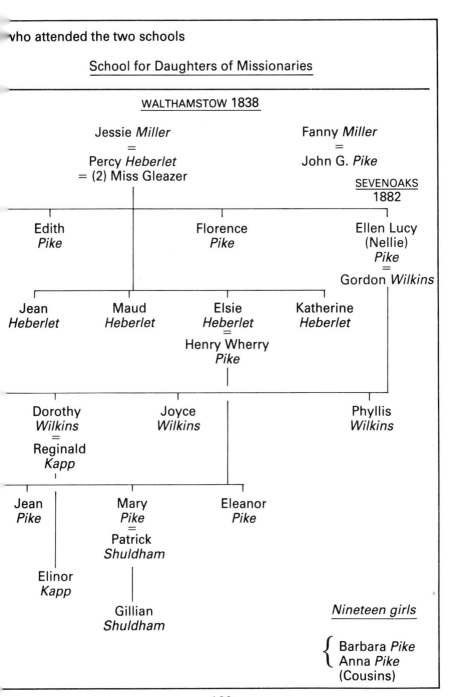

WALTHAMSTOW 1838

Jessie *Miller*
=
Percy *Heberlet*
= (2) Miss Gleazer

Fanny *Miller*
=
John G. *Pike*

SEVENOAKS
1882

Edith
Pike

Florence
Pike

Ellen Lucy
(Nellie)
Pike
=
Gordon *Wilkins*

Jean
Heberlet

Maud
Heberlet

Elsie
Heberlet
=
Henry Wherry
Pike

Katherine
Heberlet

Dorothy
Wilkins
=
Reginald
Kapp

Joyce
Wilkins

Phyllis
Wilkins

Jean
Pike

Mary
Pike
=
Patrick
Shuldham

Eleanor
Pike

Elinor
Kapp

Gillian
Shuldham

Nineteen girls

{ Barbara *Pike*
Anna *Pike*
(Cousins)

139